CHASING WINTER GOLD

MAX HITCHINS
&
JESS BRIDGER

Disclaimer:
The stories and achievements depicted in this book, Chasing Gold, are based on real-life events and the experiences of athletes who have accomplished remarkable feats. While every effort has been made to accurately portray their journeys, some creative liberties may have been taken for the sake of narrative cohesion. The intent is to inspire and celebrate the remarkable accomplishments of these athletes.

Please note that the information provided is for entertainment and informational purposes only. The author and publisher do not claim to represent the absolute truth or the complete details of each athlete's life.

Disclaimer for the Use of AI:
It is important to note that certain sections of this book utilize content generated by AI language models, including but not limited to OpenAI's GPT (Generative Pre-trained Transformer). The AI-generated content is integrated to enhance the storytelling experience and does not replace the authenticity of the athletes' achievements. The author and publisher acknowledge the contributions of AI while emphasizing that the primary focus remains on the genuine accomplishments and narratives of the athletes featured in this book.

Readers are encouraged to approach AI-generated content with an understanding of its capabilities and limitations. The utilization of AI in this book aims to explore innovative storytelling techniques while maintaining respect for the human element at the core of the featured stories.

Copyright © 2024 - by Max Hitchins
All rights reserved. No part of this book may be reproduced, distributed, or transmitted in any form or by any means, including photocopying, recording, or other electronic or mechanical methods, without the prior written permission of the publisher, except in the case of brief quotations embodied in critical reviews and certain other non-commercial uses permitted by copyright law.

Table of Contents

Welcome to Chasing Winter Gold 6

Birth of Olympic Winter Games – 1924 9

Jakara Anthony AO (AUS) Freestyle Moguls 13

Scotty James (AUS) Snowboard Halfpipe 15

Tess Coady (AUS) Snowboarding Slopestyle & Big Air 17

Valentino Guseli (AUS) Snowboard Halfpipe/Slopestyle/Big Air . 19

Belle Brockhoff (AUS) Snowboard Cross 21

Ben Tudhope (AUS) Para-Snowboard Cross SB-LL2 23

Matt Graham (AUS) Men's Moguls 25

Laura Peel (AUS) Freestyle Skiing (Aerials) 27

Danielle Scott – (AUS) - Freestyle Skiing Aerials 29

Josie Baff – (AUS) Snowboarding - Snowboard Cross 31

Breeana "Bree" Walker (Aus) Bobsleigh — Monobob & Two-Woman 33

Brendan Corey (AUS) Short Track Speed Skating 35

Steven Bradbury OAM (Australia) 38

Alisa Camplin AM (Australia) 40

Dale Begg-Smith OAM (AUSTRALIA) 42

Torah Bright OAM (AUSTRALIA) 44

Now...for a look around the world 46

Mikaela Shiffrin (USA) Alpine Skiing – Slalom & Giant Slalom 47

Chloe Kim (USA) Snowboard Halfpipe 49

Madison Chock & Evan Bates (USA) Figure Skating 51

Erin Jackson (USA) Long Track Speed Skating – 500m 53

Ilia Malinin - USA Figure Skating Men's Singles 55

Jordan Stolz (USA) Long Track Speed Skating 500/1000/1500m . 57

Johannes Høsflot Klæbo (NORWAY) Cross-Country Skiing – Sprint, Distance & Tour de Ski 59

Aleksander Aamodt Kilde (NORWAY) Alpine Skiing – Downhill & Super-G 61

Ragne Wiklund (NORWAY) Long-Track Speed – Skating 1500/3000/ /5000m 63

Marius Lindvik (NORWAY) Ski Jumping – Large Hill & Normal... 65

Francesco Friedrich (GERMANY) Bobsleigh. 2-man & 4-man. 67

Christopher Grotheer (GERMANY) Skeleton 69

Tobias Wendl & Tobias Arlt (GERMANY) Luge Doubles............... 71

Leon Draisaitl (GERMANY) - Ice Hockey Captain of Germany's national men's team for Milano-Cortina 2026 73

Andreas Wellinger (GERMANY) Ski Jumper 75

Jessica Degenhardt & Cheyenne Rosenthal (GERMANY) Women's Doubles Luge 77

Mikaël Kingsbury (CANADA) Freestyle Skiing Moguls & Dual Moguls 79

Connor McDavid (CANADA) Ice Hockey Men's Team 81

Alexandria Loutitt Ski Jumping (CANADA)................................. 83

Deanna Stellato-Dudek & Maxime Deschamps (CANADA) Figure Skating Pairs.. 85

Reece Howden – (CANADA) Freestyle Skiing Ski Cross 87

Cale Makar (CANADA) Ice Hockey Men's Team 89

About RUSSIA and Individual Neutral Athletes (AIN) 91

Adelia Petrosian (AIN) Figure Skating Women's Singles 93

Petr Gumennik (AIN) Figure Skating Men's Singles 95

Alexander Bolshunov (AIN) Cross-Country Skiing....................... 97

Alexandra Trusova (AIN) Figure Skating Women's Singles.......... 99

Anastasia Mishina & Aleksandr Galliamov (AIN) Figure Skating 101

Kamila Valieva (AIN) Figure Skating (Women's Singles) 103

Ester Ledecká (CZECH REPUBLIC) Super-G alpine skiing & snowboard parallel giant slalom.. 105

Zoi Sadowski-Synnott (NZ) Slopestyle & Big Air....................... 107

Trailblazers- Mica Moore: Making history with Jamaica Bobsleigh squad 109

Brogan Crowley, Matt Weston & Marcus Wyatt (GB) – Skeleton athletes 111

Kirsty Muir (GB) Big air & Slopestyle 113

American Rivers family (JAMAICA) representing Jamaica......... 115

Jesper Pedersen (NORWAY) Slalom Sitting................................. 117

Momoka Muraoka (JAPAN) Giant Slalom Sitting....................... 119

Giacomo Bertagnolli (ITALY) Slalom and Giant Slalom Paralympics 121

WINTER OLYMPIC CHAMPIONS... 123

Marit Bjørgen – The Queen of the Winter Olympics 124

Bonnie Blair – The Underdog Who Skated for Her Father 126

Clas Thunberg – From Rowdy Rebel to Winter Olympic Royalty 128

Sonja Henie (Norway, Figure Skating) From Ice Queen to Silver Screen Star 130

Eileen Gu (China/USA, Freestyle Skiing) 132

Johannes Thingnes Bø – 5 Olympic Gold Medals 134

Toni Sailer – Extraordinary Olympian -National hero 136

Jean-Claude Killy: From the Slopes to the Boardroom 138

Tara Lipinski: Turning Olympic Gold into a Golden Career 140

Kjetil Jansrud: The Comeback King of Norwegian Skiing............ 142

Oksana Masters: From Chernobyl's Shadow to Paralympic Glory 144

Brian McKeever: Canada's Vision of Greatness 146

Lauren Woolstencroft: Engineering Gold and Inspiring the World 148

Bibian Mentel-Spee: The Unbreakable Spirit of Paralympic Snowboarding 150

Daniel Cnossen: From the Battlefield to the Podium..................152

Oleksandra Kononova – The Orphan Who Skied into a Nation's Heart..154

Hermann Maier – The Iron Man of Alpine Skiing 156

Winter Olympic Cities 158

A Closing Reflection 162

A message from Max & Jess...163

Welcome to Chasing Winter Gold

My granddaughter Jess Bridger and I are sports devotees! For many years I've been known as Melbourne Cup Max and can tell you something about every Melbourne Cup for the last 100 years and also, something about every Summer Olympics since 1896.

Jessie is Corporate Account Manager at Allianz Stadium in Sydney, which is one of the newest state-of-the-art Stadiums in the Southern Hemisphere. Australia is one of only five nations to have competed in every Summer Olympic Games since 1896. Australia may be best known for its beaches and sunshine, but its ski fields are world-class, attracting both international tourists and elite athletes. Resorts like Perisher, Thredbo, Falls Creek and Mount Hotham offer modern facilities, extensive lift networks, high-quality snowmaking systems, and vibrant alpine villages. These venues provide excellent conditions for recreational skiers and snowboarders.

"In every conceivable manner, the family is a link to our past, a bridge to our future."
— Alex Haley

The first Aussie to compete was speed skater Kenneth Kennedy, who represented Australia solo at the 1936 Winter Olympics in Garmisch-Partenkirchen, Germany. Twelve years later, at St. Moritz in 1948, we returned with a team of three alpine skiers. But it wasn't until 1952 that Australia began its uninterrupted run of appearances at every Winter Games.

The true turning point came in 2002 at Salt Lake City, when the unthinkable happened: Steven Bradbury claimed Australia's first Winter Olympic gold in short track speed skating—a story of persistence, positioning, and perfect timing. That same year, Alisa Camplin soared to gold in the women's aerial skiing event, becoming our second Winter Olympic champion. We are especially proud to say that Alisa now serves as Chef de Mission for Australia's 2026 team in Milan-Cortina.

Since then, Australia has grown into a genuine Winter Olympics contender. For Milan-Cortina 2026, Australia is expected to send a team of around 50 athletes.

WHAT MAKES THIS BOOK UNIQUE?
Before writing *CHASING WINTER GOLD*, We asked Chat GPT"

"Has there ever been a Winter Olympics book that featured QR codes linking readers to videos about specific athletes?

ChatGPT replied:

"*Chasing Winter Gold* is the first-ever Winter Olympics book to combine the power of print with QR codes, linking readers directly to video highlights, interviews, and historic Olympic moments. Equally unique, it is the only known Winter Olympics book co-authored by a grandfather–granddaughter duo, blending generations of storytelling with cutting-edge technology. This makes Chasing Winter Gold a pioneering work in both Olympic history and publishing innovation.

Regarding books that incorporate QR codes linking directly to athlete videos, this approach is also notably rare. While some educational resources include QR-linked multimedia, they typically focus on classroom use—not storytelling or Olympic history."

That makes this book something truly special—a first-of-its-kind collaboration between a grandfather and granddaughter that brings stories of magnificent winter, summer and paralympic athletes to you, via unforgettable stories and instant access to visual highlights via QR codes.

May your enjoyment in reading and watching this book match the excitement we felt in writing and assembling it.

Birth of Olympic Winter Games – 1924

The Winter Olympic Games officially began in 1924, but their roots go back even further.

For many years, the International Olympic Committee (IOC), founded by Pierre de Coubertin in 1894, focused only on summer sports. Yet the appeal of winter sports like figure skating, ice hockey, ski jumping, and cross-country skiing continued to grow—especially in countries with strong alpine and Nordic traditions.

By the early 20th century, figure skating and ice hockey had made brief appearances in the Summer Olympics (1908 and 1920). However, athletes and sports officials began pushing for a separate international event to properly showcase cold-weather disciplines.

Their calls were answered when, in 1924, the IOC—in partnership with the French Olympic Committee—organized what was initially called *International Winter Sports Week* in the alpine town of Chamonix, France. Although it was not originally branded as the first Winter Olympics, the success of the event led the IOC to retroactively recognize it as the #1 Olympic Winter Games.

Sixteen nations took part, with around 258 athletes (245 men and 13 women) competing in six sports and 16 events. The Games included speed skating, cross-country skiing, Nordic combined, ski jumping, bobsleigh, curling, and ice hockey.

By way of comparison, here are the key figures for the 2026 Winter Olympics: 93 nations are expected to participate with over 3,500 athletes competing. The Games will feature 116 medal events across 16 disciplines within 8 sports. Notably, the 2026 Winter Olympics will introduce Ski Mountaineering as a new Olympic sport, marking its debut in the Games.

This expansion reflects the evolving nature of the Winter Olympics, showcasing a broader range of sports and greater global participation compared to the early editions of the Games.

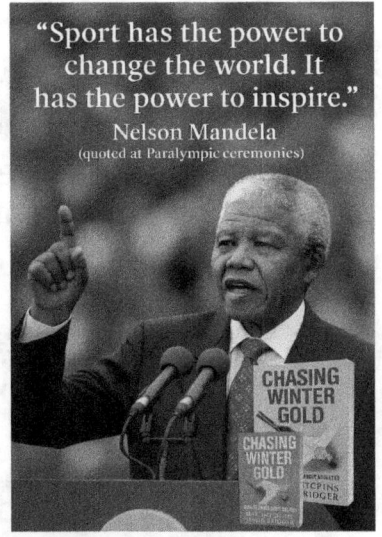

As lifelong lovers of sport, we, the authors, have been inspired by visionaries like Baron Pierre de Coubertin and Nelson Mandela. We share their belief in sport's unique power to unite people, forge lasting friendships, and even transcend conflicts.

AUSTRALIA

We openly admit to a little patriotic bias in starting our overview of possible Aussie Gold medallists. While Australia may not be a giant in winter sports, we've proven time and again that heart, grit, and a touch of daring can take you a long way – even on snow and ice!

In CHASING WINTER GOLD, we're proud to shine a spotlight on the athletes who carry the Southern Cross flag into Olympic winter history.

In this book we lead off with Australian winter sports athletes. A mix of seasoned Olympians and rising stars who are candidates to be on the medal podium at the Milano-Cortina 2026 Winter Games; We follow with details of other superb athletes from the likely top five nations; then some winter sports Trailblazers and then back to recent and past Aussie Olympians and Paralympians.

 Click on the QR code on the left to check out the Ultimate Guide to the Milano Cortina 2026 Winter Olympic Games.

Jakara Anthony AO (AUS)
Freestyle Moguls

Born 8 July 1998 in Victoria, Jakara Anthony became the first Australian to win Olympic gold in women's moguls at Beijing 2022, finishing fourth in PyeongChang 2018 (Australia's best female mogul performance until then).

She's also a World Championship silver medallist (2019) and boasts an outstanding World Cup podium haul—19 victories in a single season by late 2024.

Anthony is the reigning Olympic champion in women's moguls, having won Gold at Beijing 2022. A two-time Olympian (4th in 2018, 1st in 2022) she has become one of the world's most dominant mogul skiers. Her 2023/24 World Cup season was historic – winning 14 of 16 events and shattering records for Australian skiers. With 23 career World Cup victories to date and consistent podium finishes, Anthony is a top contender to defend her title in 2026. Jakara was awarded the Medal of the Order of Australia following her Olympic win Her combination of experience, recent dominance, and the prospect of dual moguls (a new Olympic event) gives Australia high hopes that she will once again lead the team in Milan.

Building on her dominance, Jakara is Australia's strongest gold medal threat in moguls—headlining the book and pub campaigns with stories of grit, comeback, and ambition.

"It's really incredible to know that all the hard work is really paying off. I'm just lost for words."

Jakara Anthony —
(to the Seven Network after winning in Beijing).

Did you know ski jumpers must pass a body mass index (BMI) test – too skinny and they're disqualified for safety?

Did you know?

Scotty James (AUS)
Snowboard Halfpipe

Melbourne-born (6 July 1994), Scotty James has been a trailblazer in halfpipe snowboarding. A three-time Olympian, he earned bronze in PyeongChang 2018 and silver in Beijing 2022. He's a three-time World Champion, six-time X Games winner, and four-time FIS World Cup champion.

After conquering the X Games circuit and breaking Shaun White's halfpipe record, Scotty is laser-focused on climbing the podium and claiming elusive Olympic gold.

Veteran snowboarder, James is a four-time Olympian (Vancouver 2010; Sochi 2014; Pyeong 2018 and Beijing 2022) and one of Australia's most decorated winter athletes. He owns two Olympic medals (halfpipe bronze in 2018 and silver in 2022) and has *"not much he hasn't achieved in snowboarding."* James is a three-time World Champion, a four-time Crystal Globe (World Cup) overall winner, and a seven-time X Games gold medallist in superpipe. In fact, Scotty carried Australia's flag at the 2018 opening ceremony as a testament to his leadership. The only accolade missing from James' résumé is Olympic gold, and he remains hungry to secure it.

Still in his early 30s by 2026, Scotty James' proven consistency and elite skill level make him a sure bet to represent Australia in the halfpipe once again, where he'll aim to push snowboarding to new levels and finally climb to the top of the Olympic podium.

Tess Coady (AUS) Snowboarding Slopestyle & Big Air

Tess Coady's Olympic journey began with heartbreak but has since evolved into one of Australia's most inspiring winter sports stories. Named to the national team for the 2018 PyeongChang Winter Games as a teenage sensation, her dreams were put on hold after a devastating knee injury during training ruled her out before she could compete. The setback kept her out of the 2018–2019 season entirely, forcing a long and difficult rehabilitation.

But Coady's comeback was nothing short of remarkable. Returning to the World Cup circuit in the 2019–2020 season, she quickly reestablished herself as one of the world's most stylish and technically gifted riders. Her persistence paid off in spectacular fashion at the Beijing 2022 Winter Olympics, where she captured bronze in women's slopestyle—a historic medal for Australia and a personal triumph over adversity.

Since Beijing, Coady has built on her success with an impressive series of results. At the 2021 FIS World Championships, she claimed bronze in slopestyle, followed by bronze in big air at the 2023 World Championships. She has also proven her skill on the sport's most prestigious stage outside the Olympics, earning an X Games silver medal, further cementing her place among snowboarding's elite.

Coady's riding style is defined by smooth execution, creative lines, and a rapidly growing arsenal of high-difficulty tricks. Her technical progression, combined with her ability to perform under pressure, keeps her in contention against the sport's strongest competitors. Off the slopes, she is known for her positive attitude, resilience, and as a role model for young athletes overcoming setbacks.

Valentino Guseli (AUS) Snowboard Halfpipe/Slopestyle/Big Air

Born on April 1, 2005, in the Australian Capital Territory, Valentino Guseli has rapidly become one of the most exciting names in snowboarding. Bursting onto the Olympic stage at just 16, he impressed the world with a 6th-place finish in the halfpipe at Beijing 2022, showcasing a rare mix of style, power, and fearlessness beyond his years.

Since then, Guseli's rise has been nothing short of meteoric. In 2022, he stunned the sport by breaking the world record for the highest halfpipe air, cementing his reputation as a boundary-pushing innovator. The momentum didn't stop there—by 2023, he claimed silver at the World Championships in halfpipe and added multiple World Cup podium finishes across three disciplines. In 2024, his consistency and all-around brilliance earned him a Crystal Globe, solidifying his place among the sport's elite.

What sets Guseli apart is his "triple-threat" status—an exceptionally rare feat in modern snowboarding. While most riders specialize in a single discipline, Guseli competes at the highest level in halfpipe, slopestyle, and big air, bringing a complete park-and-pipe arsenal to every event. This versatility has sparked his boldest goal yet: to become the first male snowboarder to compete in all three park-and-pipe events at a single Olympic Games.

His journey hasn't been without setbacks. In 2024, a knee injury threatened to derail his progress, but Guseli attacked rehab with the same determination he shows on the snow. Now fully focused on Milano-Cortina 2026, his recovery has only deepened his hunger for Olympic success.

Beyond the stats and medals, Guseli's dynamic riding style—defined by huge amplitude, technical rotations, and creative line choices makes him a crowd favourite. His Italian heritage ensures he'll enjoy plenty of home-nation support in Cortina.

Belle Brockhoff (AUS) Snowboard Cross

Belle Brockhoff was born 12 January 1993 in Victoria. She is a three-time Olympian (2014, 2018, 2022), 2021 World Championship team gold medallist in snowboard cross.

After enduring a shattered wrist that made even seasoned surgeons wince, Australian snowboard cross star Belle Brockhoff is back on snow – restarting her campaign toward Milano-Cortina 2026, almost one year to the day before the Olympic cauldron is lit.

Now 32, Brockhoff is no stranger to injury. From competing without an ACL in PyeongChang 2018 to finishing fourth in Beijing 2022 with her knee duct-taped and braced, she has shown extraordinary toughness. But the 2023 wrist break was a harsh reminder of the risks of her sport.

Still, Brockhoff refuses to be distracted by Olympic dreams. "I focus on the 'now'—on recovery, on each day of training. Looking too far ahead causes anxiety," she says. But don't mistake focus for lack of ambition.

Belle's mindset has evolved. Once crushed by anything less than gold, she now values performance over podiums. "I'd rather ride flawlessly and come fourth than win riding poorly," she explains.

Supported by her family, partner Georgia, coach John Povey, and performance psychologist Caroline Anderson, Brockhoff credits her team with keeping her grounded and resilient.

Why does she keep coming back? "Because when it's good, it's really good," she smiles. "It's like a rollercoaster. And when I shout 'Whoo-hoo!' down the course—that's the feeling I chase."

"To compete for Australia is an honour. An Olympic medal? That's the dream."

Belle Brockhoff

Ben Tudhope (AUS)
Para-Snowboard Cross SB-LL2

Ben Tudhope is Australia's youngest-ever Winter Paralympian. He debuted at age 14 in 2014).

Ben Tudhope's story begins long before the podium lights. Born in December 1999 in Manly, NSW, with hemiplegic cerebral palsy affecting his left side. He found joy and freedom on snow from a young age—first skiing at age three, then inspired by his older sister he switched to snowboarding. His talent was clear early on and at just fourteen, in Sochi 2014 he carried the flag at the Closing Ceremony.

Fast forward to Beijing 2022, where Tudhope delivered a thrilling performance to claim bronze in snowboard cross SB-LL2, securing Australia's first Winter Paralympic medal of the Games. His perseverance was rewarded once more in 2023, when he earned gold in snowboard cross at the World Para Snowboard Championships in La Molina. On the World Cup circuit, Tudhope has been a powerhouse, winning multiple races and earning overall SB-LL2 and overall Snowboard Crystal Globes FIS Ski and Snowboard.

He was also named Male Athlete of the Year in Paralympic Disciplines at the Snow Australia Awards—his seventh consecutive title by 2025—

emphasizing a consistency rooted in both skill and joy.

Heading into Milano–Cortina 2026, Tudhope will be Australia's Para-Snowboard Co-Captain, leading from both the start gate and the heart with experience, humility, and ambition. He represents not just elite athleticism but also the power of self-belief and disability inclusion—a true role model for aspiring athletes.

Matt Graham (AUS) Men's Moguls

Matt Graham has been a cornerstone of Australia's freestyle skiing program for more than a decade, bringing a mix of technical mastery, competitive grit, and remarkable consistency to the mogul's course. Milano-Cortina 2026 on the horizon, will be his fourth Olympic appearance, a rare milestone in Australian winter sport.

Graham's Olympic journey began in Sochi 2014, but it was at PyeongChang 2018, that he etched his name into history. There, he delivered a brilliant performance to win silver in men's moguls, Australia's first-ever medal in this event. That breakthrough cemented his reputation as one of the sport's elites.

His career boasts four World Championship medals in moguls' events, a testament to his ability to perform at his peak when the stakes are highest. In 2021, Graham claimed the overall World Cup title (Crystal Globe) in moguls, further underscoring his place among the world's best.

The road to Beijing 2022 was far from smooth— Graham suffered a broken collarbone just weeks before the Games. Yet, in a show of determination and resilience, he competed in his third Olympics despite the injury.

The effort only reinforced his standing as one of Australia's toughest winter athletes.

Since then, Graham has returned to top form, racking up multiple World Cup podiums and even achieving dual victories alongside Olympic champion Jakara Anthony, highlighting the strength of Australia's mogul squad. His 2025 season added another accolade—a World Championship medal—proving he remains at the forefront of the sport.

Milano-Cortina presents a new opportunity: the addition of dual moguls to the Olympic program. For Graham, this means not just one, but two chances to add to his Olympic medal tally.

Laura Peel (AUS) Freestyle Skiing (Aerials)

Laura Peel stands as one of Australia's most accomplished aerial skiers, with a career defined by daring feats, remarkable consistency, and an unwavering pursuit of excellence. When she takes the stage in Milano-Cortina 2026, it will mark her fourth Olympic Games, cementing her status as a legend of Australian winter sport.

Peel's resume is glittered with achievements. She is a two-time World Champion in women's aerials, claiming titles in 2015 and 2021, and has earned three career Crystal Globes as the overall World Cup aerials champion, the most recent coming in the 2024–25 season. Over her career, she has amassed 14 World Cup victories, consistently delivering under the highest pressure.

What sets Peel apart is her mastery of the triple-twisting triple backflip—one of the most difficult jumps in the sport and one attempted by only a select few women worldwide. It's a skill that has brought her victories and made her a constant threat to any podium she contests.

In Olympic competition, Peel has come agonisingly close to a medal, finishing 5th in both PyeongChang 2018 and Beijing 2022. Yet, instead of deterring her, those results have fuelled her drive.

In recent seasons, she has continued to push the boundaries, landing her signature triple-twisting somersault to win the Olympic test event in Italy.

Now in her mid-30s, Peel has shown that age is no barrier to innovation and elite performance. Her experience, technical skill, and proven ability to rise to big moments make her an invaluable leader for the Australian team heading into Milano-Cortina.

For Peel, the goal in 2026 is clear: to capture the one accolade missing from her illustrious career—an Olympic medal.

"Honestly the second time feels even better... I saved my best for the final... I am so happy to put it down."

Laura Peel

Danielle Scott – (AUS) - Freestyle Skiing Aerials

Danielle Scott is a name synonymous with excellence in aerial skiing. A veteran of three Olympic Games—Sochi 2014, PyeongChang 2018, and Beijing 2022. Scott is preparing for what will be her fourth Olympic appearance at Milano-Cortina 2026. Over more than a decade at the sport's elite level, she has built a reputation for consistency, athleticism, and the courage to perform the sport's most challenging tricks.

Scott's resume is one of Australia's most decorated in Winter sport. She has earned four World Championship medals, including silvers in 2017 and 2023 and bronzes in 2013 and 2025. In recent years, she has taken her performance to new heights, securing back-to-back World Cup Crystal Globe titles as the season's overall champion in 2022–23 and 2023–24—an achievement that confirms her as the world's top-ranked female aerialist.

Known for executing technically demanding triple backflips, Scott's competition runs combine power and precision. Her dominance on the World Cup circuit over the past two seasons has been marked by multiple wins and podium finishes, proving she is competing at the peak of her career.

Her Olympic journey has had highs and challenges. At Beijing 2022, Scott faced tough conditions and finished 10th—short of her medal ambitions—but she rebounded with resilience. The seasons that followed have been the strongest of her career, underscoring her readiness to contend for an Olympic podium.

Scott's drive is not just about personal glory; she continues a proud tradition of Australian excellence in aerial skiing, following in the footsteps of legends like Alisa Camplin and Lydia Lassila.

Josie Baff – (AUS) Snowboarding - Snowboard Cross

Josie Baff has quickly become one of the brightest talents in Australian winter sport, blazing a trail in snowboard cross and redefining what's possible for the nation's snowboarding scene. At just 17 years old, Baff made history at the 2020 Winter Youth Olympic Games in Lausanne, winning gold in women's snowboard cross—the first Australian to claim a title at the event.

Her transition to senior competition was equally impressive. By 2022, she had earned a spot on the Beijing Winter Olympic team, where she competed in both the women's event and the mixed team competition. While her 18th-place finish in the individual event was a learning experience, it provided a valuable foundation for what was to come.

Baff's rise since Beijing has been nothing short of meteoric. In 2023, she claimed silver at the Snowboard Cross World Championships—a historic first for Australia in the event—and solidified her place among the world's elite riders. That breakthrough was no fluke. Over the next two seasons, she amassed 11 World Cup podium finishes by early 2025, including multiple silver medals in a single season.

Her performance consistency placed her third overall in the World Cup standings.

What sets Baff apart is her fearless approach to racing. Snowboard cross is one of the most unpredictable and physically demanding events in the Winter Games, yet Baff's ability to remain composed in high-pressure heats has made her a constant threat for the podium. Her knack for explosive starts, smooth transitions, and tactical passing gives her an edge against seasoned veterans.

Breeana "Bree" Walker (Aus)
Bobsleigh — Monobob & Two-Woman

Bree Walker has carved her name into Australian winter sports history, emerging as the nation's most successful bobsleigh pilot. Her Olympic debut at Beijing 2022 was a breakthrough moment—not only for her career but for Australian sliding sports—when she claimed 5th place in the inaugural Women's Monobob event. It was an extraordinary result for an athlete from a country with almost no bobsleigh tradition.

A former track sprinter, Walker transitioned into bobsleigh with remarkable speed, displaying the explosive power and precision steering needed to succeed in a discipline dominated by North American and European teams. Over the past few seasons, she has built an impressive résumé, with more than 10 World Cup podiums to her name. The highlight came in early 2024 at Lake Placid, where she made history by becoming the first Australian to win a Bobsleigh World Cup gold in the Women's Monobob.

Her 2023–24 season cemented her place among the sport's elite. Walker finished ranked #2 in the world in the overall Monobob standings, consistently challenging for medals and picking up a string of silvers and bronzes along the way.

Walker is equally determined in the two-woman bobsleigh, where she teams up with brake woman Kiara Reddingius. The duo placed 16th at Beijing 2022 after only a few races together, but their growing experience offers promise for Milano-Cortina 2026.

With her trailblazing World Cup victory and proven ability to match the best in the world, Bree Walker will lead Australia's small but determined bobsleigh contingent in Italy. While the sport's traditional giants will start as favourites, Walker's recent form ensures she will arrive in Milan as a genuine outside medal chance—and a symbol of how far Australian sliding sports have come.

'The body achieves what the mind believes.'

Brendan Corey (AUS)
Short Track Speed Skating

Brendan Corey is at the forefront of a new era for Australian short track speed skating. At Beijing 2022, he stood alone as Australia's sole short track representative, battling against the sport's traditional powerhouses. Despite the challenge, Corey impressed, reaching the quarterfinals and finishing 15th in the men's 1000m and 21st in the 500m.

That Olympic experience laid the foundation for a remarkable rise. In March 2024, Corey achieved a milestone that shook Australian skating history—winning a bronze medal in the 1500m at the World Short Track Championships. It was Australia's first individual world championship medal in short track in over three decades, a feat last seen during the era of Steven Bradbury.

This podium wasn't just a personal triumph; it was the best Australian result in the sport since Bradbury's legendary 2002 Olympic gold. Brendan now regularly ranks in the world's top 10 and has broken multiple national records, showcasing his speed, race craft, and resilience.

His path to success is built on relentless training, strategic racing, and the ability to adapt to the unpredictable nature of short track—where races are won not only by speed but by split-second decisions. Now in his mid-20s, Corey is entering the prime of his career. With the Milano-Cortina 2026 Winter Olympics on the horizon, he has a clear goal: to convert his World Championship success into an Olympic medal.

"I still feel like I'm dreaming – I went all out until the end. That's what short track is all about, crazy racing and who can do it on the day."

Brendan Corey

Australia's history at the Winter Olympics is still young compared to the great snow nations of the world, yet it has already produced shining moments of inspiration. From Steven Bradbury's unforgettable triumph in Salt Lake City (2002), to Alisa Camplin's daring aerials in the same year, Dale Begg-Smith's moguls mastery in 2006, Torah Bright's golden halfpipe run in 2010, Lydia Lasilla's flawless triple-twisting double somersault GOLD MEDAL winning effort and Jakara Anthony's brilliance in freestyle skiing at Beijing 2022 (see page 13).

These athletes broke new ground for Australia on the world stage. They proved that Australians could rise to the top on the world's snow and ice.

Steven Bradbury OAM (Australia)

Steven Bradbury's journey in the world of short track speed skating, is a tale of resilience, setbacks, and ultimately, an unexpected triumph that would secure his place in Olympic history.

In 1991, Bradbury contributed to Australia's first-ever world championship in a winter sport, winning the 5,000-metre relay at the World Championships in Sydney. However, his Olympic path was marred by crashes and injuries in subsequent years, including a devastating neck fracture in a training accident in 2000 that could have killed him.

Against all odds and medical advice, Bradbury was determined to reach another Olympics. His perseverance led him to the Salt Lake City 2002 Winter Olympics, where he faced formidable opponents in the men's short track 1000 metres event.

In the quarter finals, a disqualification and unexpected crashes by top skaters paved the way for Bradbury's entry into the final. In a spectacular turn of events at the last corner of the race, all his competitors crashed, creating an opportunity for Bradbury to seize victory.

Bradbury's gold medal win, though unconventional, turned him into a folk hero. His triumph resonated beyond the sporting world, embodying the spirit of an underdog who never gave up.

Beyond the Olympic arena, Bradbury's life took a new trajectory. From needing financial support for his training to becoming a sought-after figure for sponsorships and television interviews, he transformed from a skater making boots in a backyard workshop to a National inspiring celebrity.

Steven Bradbury's story is not just about winning a gold medal. It's about overcoming adversity, defying expectations, and leaving a legacy in the annals of Australian sporting history. His autobiography is called **'Last Man Standing'**.

Alisa Camplin AM (Australia)

Alisa Camplin AM is an Australian aerial skier born on 10 November 1974. She has left an indelible mark on the winter sports landscape, earning her a place among Australia's finest athletes. Her journey is highlighted by her gold medal triumph at the 2002 Winter Olympics, making her the second Australian to achieve this feat in the history of the games.

Standing at 157 cm tall, Camplin's early life saw her excel in gymnastics before transitioning to aerial skiing. Educated at Melbourne's Methodist Ladies' College, she holds a bachelor's degree in information technology from Swinburne University of Technology.

Camplin's path to success was not without challenges. Prior to the 2002 Winter Olympics, she faced numerous injuries, including a broken collarbone, broken hand, separated shoulder, two broken ankles, torn Achilles tendon, torn ACL, and nine concussions.

In the 2002 Winter Olympics at Salt Lake City, Camplin competed against doctors' advice, discovering only upon examination in Salt Lake City that both her ankles were fractured. Undeterred, she delivered a stunning performance to secure the gold medal. Her victory not only made her the first Australian skier to win consecutive Winter Olympic medals but also earned her a commemorative 45-cent stamp from Australia Post.

Camplin's journey continued to the 2006 Winter Olympics in Turin, where she faced a serious knee injury. Despite a third-place finish, her tenacity and dedication to the sport were evident.

The proud moment Max met Alisa Camplin in 2012.

In July 2006, Camplin announced her retirement from competition, pivoting towards a successful post-skiing career. As of 2024, she is an international executive for IBM, a motivational speaker, and a senior executive managing a team of over 300 people.

Dale Begg-Smith OAM (AUSTRALIA)

Begg-Smith's journey was unconventional. A teenage internet entrepreneur, he and his brother Jason relocated from Canada to Australia at age 16 to balance business and training in a smaller ski program.

After three years of honing their craft in Jindabyne, gaining Australian citizenship, he climbed to the top of the world rankings in moguls.

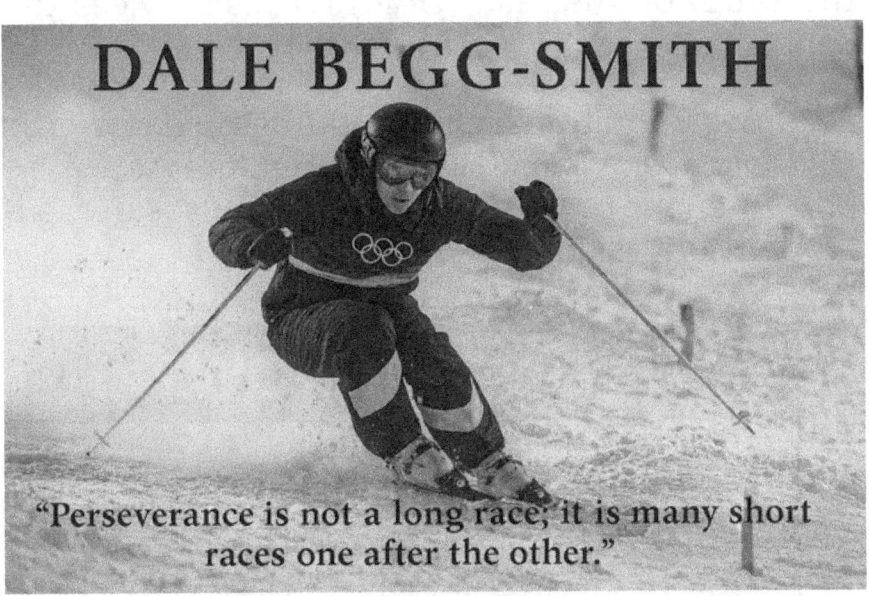

"Perseverance is not a long race; it is many short races one after the other."

In Turin, in 2006, his final run in the men's moguls was near-flawless—audacious turns, controlled air, precision speed—earning him a commanding lead over the field.

Four years later, in Vancouver 2010, he added silver to his tally, narrowly edged out by Canada's Alexandre Bilodeau in a tight final. Despite losing gold, he remained Australia's most decorated Winter Olympian at that point.

Beyond the medals, Begg-Smith left a lasting legacy. Between 2005 and 2010, he notched 18 World Cup wins, four crystal globes, and stood on the podium 29 times. In 2018, he was awarded the Medal of the Order of Australia (OAM) for his services to sport.

Dale Begg-Smith transformed Australia's Winter Olympic aspirations. His rise from internet entrepreneur to world-beating moguls' skier is a story of grit, skill, and audacity.

DID YOU KNOW?

Did you know the 2022 Beijing Games made it the first city ever to host both Summer and Winter Olympics?

Torah Bright OAM (AUSTRALIA)

Torah Jane Bright OAM, born on 27th December 1986 in Cooma, New South Wales, redefined Australia's winter sports legacy as its most successful female Winter Olympian ever. A fearless snowboarder, she first graced the Olympic stage at Torino 2006, narrowly missing the podium with a fifth-place finish in halfpipe—just one point shy. Her defining moment arrived at the 2010 Vancouver Winter Olympics.

Selected as Australia's flag-bearer, she battled through injury and the pressure of the opening ceremony to claim gold in the women's halfpipe. After crashing on her first run, she composed herself and produced a stunning second run—scoring 45.0, the highest of the night—and earned gold as no one could surpass her score.

Bright sustained her momentum into the 2014 Sochi Games, where she made history as the first Olympic athlete—regardless of gender—to compete in all three snowboarding disciplines: halfpipe, slopestyle, and snowboard cross. She added a silver medal in halfpipe to her collection, narrowly missing back-to-back golds.

Bright's achievements include multiple X Games golds, US Opens, Global Opens, World Superpipe

Championships, and a TTR World Tour title—making her an icon of snowboarding. In 2012, she was awarded the Medal of the Order of Australia (OAM), and in August 2025 she was inducted into the Sport Australia Hall of Fame, cementing her place in the nation's sporting history.

"THE HARDER THE CONFLICT, THE GREATER THE TRIUMPH."
– GEORGE WASHINGTON

Torah Bright's journey—from a skiing toddler in the Snowy Mountains to Olympic champion and Hall-of-Famer—is one of grit, adaptability, and groundbreaking achievement.

Now...for a look around the world

Throughout history, the Winter Olympics have been dominated by traditional medal powerhouses such as the USA, Norway, Germany, Canada, and Russia. In preparing this section, we have carefully examined the achievements of standout athletes from these nations, whose performances have set benchmarks of excellence. At the same time, it is essential to acknowledge the growing influence of countries such as the Czech Republic, New Zealand, China, and Great Britain, whose athletes are emerging as formidable contenders on the world stage.

In preparing this section, we have undertaken detailed research into standout athletes from these countries. At the same time, it is equally important to highlight the exceptional talent emerging from other nations such as the Czech Republic, New Zealand, China, and Great Britain, whose athletes are making a significant impact.

USA

Mikaela Shiffrin (USA)
Alpine Skiing – Slalom & Giant Slalom

Mikaela Shiffrin isn't just one of the greatest skiers of her generation—she may be the greatest of all time. Born in Colorado in 1995, Shiffrin burst onto the world stage as a teenage prodigy. At just 18 years old, she became the youngest-ever Olympic gold medallist in Slalom at the Sochi 2014 Winter Games. Four years later, she claimed a second Olympic Gold in giant slalom at PyeongChang 2018, adding to a career that has since shattered records.

As of 2025, she has achieved an astonishing 101 World Cup victories, more than any other alpine skier in history—male or female. With multiple World Cup overall titles, Shiffrin's dominance in slalom and giant slalom is matched only by her consistency, technical brilliance, and mental toughness.

Yet her journey has not been without setbacks. After a challenging Olympics in Beijing 2022, where she failed to finish in multiple events, Shiffrin returned to the sport with fierce determination. Her resilience and humility have endeared her to fans worldwide.

Now, heading into her fourth Olympic Games in Milano-Cortina 2026, Mikaela is more focused than ever. As Team USA's top medal hope, she stands not just as a symbol of American alpine skiing but as an inspiration to athletes everywhere. Her pursuit of excellence continues to raise the bar for the sport.

Shiffrin's blend of youthful fire and veteran wisdom makes her a force to watch. With dual threats in slalom and giant slalom, she is a genuine contender for gold. But beyond the medals, Mikaela represents grace under pressure,

relentless pursuit, and the courage to rise after falling. We invite you to scan the QR code, on the left, to witness Michaela 'do a deal' with Kelsey Ballerini and Michael Bublé about skiing and singing!

DID YOU KNOW?

Did you know in 1988, Jamaica sent its first bobsleigh team despite never having snow at home?
(Cool Runnings anyone?)

Chloe Kim (USA) Snowboard Halfpipe

At just 17, Chloe Kim launched herself into history with a dazzling, high-flying performance in the women's halfpipe final at the PyeongChang 2018 Winter Olympics. Calm, focused, and fearless, she became the youngest female snowboarder to win Olympic gold, instantly capturing the world's imagination and redefining what it meant to be a champion.

Her face soon appeared on cereal boxes, global magazine covers, and late-night talk shows. Even Frances McDormand gave her a shout-out at the Oscars. But behind the headlines and the hype, Chloe stayed true to herself. In a courageous move, she stepped away from competition to focus on her mental well-being and began studying at Princeton University.

After nearly two years off the snow, doubts lingered. But in Beijing 2022, Chloe silenced the critics—and soared once more. Her winning run was a reminder that this was not just an elite athlete, but a once-in-a-generation phenomenon. With her second gold medal secured, Chloe etched her name into Olympic history once again.

Now, she's chasing something never done before: a three-peat. At the Milano-Cortina 2026 Games, Chloe Kim has the chance to become the first snowboarder to win three Olympic gold medals in the halfpipe.

Chloe Kim's story is about more than gold medals—it's about balance, bravery, and blazing a trail for future generations. She's proof that greatness comes not just from winning, but from staying true to yourself.

We invite you to click the QR code, on the left, to a see Today Show USA interview with Chloe after winning her first Gold Medal.

Madison Chock & Evan Bates (USA)
Figure Skating

For over a decade, Madison Chock and Evan Bates have skated their way into the hearts of fans around the world—equal parts athletic excellence and artistic mastery.

Their journey began in 2011 when they teamed up on the ice. From promising early performances to agonising near-misses, the pair's story reached a new high in 2023 when they won their first World Championship title. But that was just the beginning. Skating out of their adopted home base in Montreal, they went on to win back-to-back titles in 2024 and 2025, becoming the first ice dance team in almost 30 years to earn a World Championship three-peat.

Their style is powerful, poetic, and technically flawless. Chock and Bates are known for their bold choreography, emotional storytelling, and a deep connection that elevates every performance.

At the Beijing 2022 Winter Olympics, they helped Team USA win gold in the team figure skating event—cementing their Olympic legacy. They've also equalled the U.S. record with six national titles, standing shoulder to shoulder with American greats Meryl Davis and Charlie White.

Their recent dominance extended to the Grand Prix circuit, where they won consecutive Grand Prix Final titles in the 2023–24 and 2024–25 seasons—testament to their resilience and continual reinvention.

What makes their story even more compelling is their bond off the rink. Romantically linked since 2017, they were engaged in 2022 and married in Hawaii in 2024. Their personal love story mirrors their professional unity—two lives, one shared dream.

As they prepare for what may be their final Olympic appearance, Chock and Bates remain the team to beat in Italy in 2026. With double gold in their sights—individual and team events—they skate not just for medals, but to finish a fairytale on their own terms.

DID YOU KNOW?

Did you know Sonja Henie was just 11 when she competed in figure skating at the 1924 Games?

Erin Jackson (USA)
Long Track Speed Skating – 500m

Erin Jackson's journey to Olympic gold didn't begin on frozen lakes in the Alps or Nordic mountains—it started on wheels, under the sun, in Ocala, Florida.

A former inline skating champion and roller derby star, Jackson only stepped onto the ice for the first time in 2016. Within six years, she did what no other black woman had ever done at a Winter Olympics: win an individual gold medal.

At the Beijing 2022 Games, Jackson scorched the 500m oval in 37.04 seconds, winning gold and ending a 28-year U.S. medal drought in the women's sprint event. Her victory wasn't just fast—it was historic. She became the first African American woman to win Olympic speed skating gold, breaking through both time barriers and racial ones.

But her rise wasn't without drama. In the U.S. Olympic trials leading up to Beijing, Jackson slipped and missed qualifying—until teammate Brittany Bowe selflessly gave up her spot so Jackson could compete. The gesture sparked headlines; the gold medal that followed became legend.

Since Beijing, Jackson has dominated the World Cup circuit, claiming multiple 500m season titles and firmly establishing herself as the fastest woman on ice.

Now 32, she heads into Milano-Cortina 2026 as the defending Olympic champion, with the same drive, humility, and heart that made her a fan favourite across the globe.

Jackson is more than a medal contender—she's a symbol of what's possible. Her story inspires young athletes from underrepresented communities and reminds the world that talent, when given the chance, can thrive anywhere— even from a roller rink in Florida.

Ilia Malinin - USA
Figure Skating Men's Singles

At just 20 years old, Ilia Malinin has already rewritten the history books of figure skating. Hailing from Fairfax, Virginia, the son of two former Olympic skaters, Malinin is widely known by his social media handle Quadg0d—a nod to his breakthrough technical mastery.

In September 2022, aged 17, he stunned the skating world by landing the quadruple Axel—a 4.5-revolution jump previously deemed impossible—in international competition. That moment cemented his reputation as the most gifted jumper of his era.

In spring 2024, Malinin took his next giant leap. At the World Championships in Montreal, he executed six quadruple jumps—including the quad Axel—in his free skate, earning a record free-skate score of 227.79 and a combined total of 333.76 to claim his first world title. This historic performance made him the second man ever to land six quads in one program—and the first to do so with a quad Axel.

He followed up that triumph with a dominant season: another world championship in Boston 2025, leading the short program with a personal-best 110.41 score and skating clean in his free skate to become a two-time world champion

Alongside, he has captured multiple Grand Prix Final titles and three U.S. national championships (2023, 2024, 2025).

Now eyeing his first Olympic Games, Malinin enters Milano-Cortina 2026 as the clear favourite in men's singles. Having missed the 2022 Beijing Olympics due to age ineligibility, he arrives in Italy smarter, steadier, and more mature pressurized not by podiums won but by future legacy.

With his parents and coach team—including Rafael Arutyunian—finalizing routines that balance artistic finesse with technical innovation, Malinin aims to skate seven quadruple jumps without unnecessary risk in Milan—and perhaps take skating into new territory with a quintuple in the future. As Quad God, he stands on the threshold of Olympic gold—ready to elevate the sport and claim his place in history.

DID YOU KNOW?

Did you know women were only allowed to compete in figure skating in 1924?

Jordan Stolz (USA) Long Track Speed Skating 500/1000/1500m

From the frozen backyard pond in Wisconsin to the top of the world stage, Jordan Stolz's journey is the stuff of legends. Inspired by watching the 2010 Winter Olympics on television, he first strapped on skates at age five—at his father's ice-lit backyard pond—and never looked back.

At just 17, Stolz became the third-youngest American male to compete in Olympic speed skating at Beijing 2022, finishing 13th and 14th in the 500 m and 1000 m respectively.

But 2023 marked a turning point: in Heerenveen, he claimed all three sprint titles—500 m, 1000 m, and 1500 m—at the World Single Distances Championships, making him the youngest male world champion in history and the first man ever to sweep those three distances at a single championship event.

He repeated the feat in 2024 in Calgary, setting national and track records along the way. Stolz also broke the world record in the big combination at the World All-round Championships, becoming the youngest since Eric Heiden to take that title—echoing U.S. speed skating greatness.

The 2025 World Championships in Hamar brought three more medals—two silvers and a bronze—

narrowly beaten by world-class competitors in tight races.

At just 20, Stolz is already drawing comparisons to Eric Heiden, the only American to win more than two Golds at a single Winter Olympics. If Jordan can replicate his World Championships dominance in Italy, he'd cement himself as one of the sport's all-time greats. His rise from backyard skater to world record holder is more than breathtaking—it's a sign that American speed skating has a champion who's rewriting the record books and redefining legacy.

NORWAY

Johannes Høsflot Klæbo (NORWAY)
Cross-Country Skiing – Sprint, Distance & Tour de Ski

Johannes Høsflot Klæbo has long defined excellence in cross-country skiing. Born in Oslo in 1996, Klæbo entered on skis with pedigree—his grandfather Kåre was his coach, his father his manager—and quickly broke ground. He was the youngest male ever to win the overall World Cup, Tour de Ski, an Olympic gold, and a World Championship title Fastest Skier.

At just 21, he stormed Beijing 2018, winning three Olympic gold medals in sprint, team sprint and relay events, tying the US biathlon legend Martin Fourcade for most golds at a single Games. In the seasons that followed, Klæbo cemented his dominance by capturing multiple Crystal Globes, sprint and distance titles and racking up more than 96 World Cup victories through 2025.

At the 2025 World Championships in Trondheim, Klæbo produced one of the most astonishing performances in Cross-Country history: winning all six men's events—including sprint, 10 km classic, skiathlon, team sprint, relay and the gruelling 50 km mass-start freestyle. With six gold medals over as many races, he surpassed Petter Northug to become the most decorated male athlete in the history of the World Championships.

Only days earlier, he had claimed Gold in the 10 km classic (his 12th world title), showcasing tactical mastery in freezing, snowy conditions. In the team sprint, Klæbo anchored Norway to a commanding win, securing a fourth gold.

Elsewhere on the circuit, Klæbo clinched his fifth overall Crystal Globe in 2025 after sweeping the sprint titles and extending his streak to 16 consecutive World Cup sprint wins. He also claimed the Tour de Ski crown for the fourth time in early 2025, confirming refusal of any challenger's momentum. As the 2026 Winter Olympics approach, Klæbo enters the picture as the undisputed favourite.

DID YOU KNOW?

Did you know the Olympic torch was once carried by a diver underwater in the 2014 Sochi relay?

Aleksander Aamodt Kilde (NORWAY)
Alpine Skiing – Downhill & Super-G

Aleksander Aamodt Kilde is synonymous with speed, strength and unshakeable determination. Crowned the 2020 overall World Cup champion, he has racked up more than 21 career victories in speed events—downhill and super-G—placing him among alpine skiing's elite.

At the Beijing 2022 Winter Olympics, Kilde earned silver in alpine combined and bronze in Super-G—adding prestigious Olympic hardware to his résumé.

In January 2024, Kilde crashed violently during the legendary Lauberhorn downhill in Wengen at speeds exceeding 100 km/h. The crash left him with torn shoulder ligaments, a deep calf laceration and nerve damage—and then an infection that escalated to life-threatening sepsis, requiring emergency surgery in Colorado and further reconstruction in Innsbruck using grafts from his hamstring and trapezius.

He missed the entire 2024–25 World Cup season during rehabilitation—never racing but slowly rebuilding strength. He described being limited to 30-minute walks with his arm in a sling and needing repeated surgeries.

Now 32, Kilde has quietly returned to training and hopes to race again at Beaver Creek in December 2025, which would officially mark his comeback on the World Cup circuit. His goal is clear: his first Olympic Gold medal in downhill or super-G in Milan-Cortina.

"If I'm back in Beaver Creek, the Olympics can follow—but first you must qualify," he said

What defines Kilde isn't just podiums or titles; it's his refusal to be sidelined. His journey from catastrophic crash to hopeful return is a testament to resilience, mental strength, and unwavering belief. With the support of fiancée Mikaela Shiffrin and his recovery team, Kilde is poised to sprint back onto the world stage.

DID YOU KNOW?

Did you know Eddie "The Eagle" Edwards became more famous for finishing last in ski jumping (1988) than many of the winners?

Ragne Wiklund (NORWAY) Long-Track Speed – Skating 1500/3000//5000m

Emerging from Oslo, Ragne Wiklund quickly developed a dual identity: elite speed skater and national orienteering champion. But it was on ice that she made history.

At the 2021 World Single Distances Championships in Heerenveen, Wiklund became the first Norwegian woman to win the world title in the 1500 m, clocking a personal best of 1:54.61, outpacing world-class rivals Brittany Bowe and Evgeniia Lalenkova.

That win ushered in a new chapter in Norwegian women's speed skating, one previously dominated almost exclusively by men.

Since then, Wiklund has evolved into a powerful and versatile middle- to long-distance skater. She has collected multiple World Cup victories, especially in the 3000 m and 5000 m events, consistently standing on the podium in international competitions.

At the 2025 World Single Distances Championships in Hamar, she claimed silver in the 5000 m, finishing just 0.18 seconds behind Francesca Lollobrigida in a dramatic race on home ice.

Then, at the 2025 World Cup season, she recorded personal bests—including a standout 3000 m time of 3:54.86 in Milwaukee and a 1500 m of 1:53.81 in the same venue, establishing national records and topping the stats in long distances.

At 25 years old, Wiklund is Norway's leading hope for a first-ever Olympic medal in long-distance racing. She brings not only pace and precision, but also mental resilience, a reflection of talents honed both on the ice and in the Norwegian forests, where she also excels in orienteering.

Wiklund enters Milan–Cortina 2026 as a respected podium threat in the 1500 m and 3000 m/5000 m events. With her national records, unique finishing speed, and championship experience, she embodies a new era of Norwegian women's skating.

Ragne Wiklund isn't just racing the clock—she's racing history!

Marius Lindvik (NORWAY)
Ski Jumping – Large Hill & Normal

Marius Lindvik has a flair for flying—and the results to prove it. Born in 1998 and raised in Rælingen, Norway, Lindvik emerged through the ranks of the sport's powerhouse nation with fierce consistency and a calm head under pressure. While many ski jumpers peak young and flame out early, Lindvik's rise has been measured, strong, and spectacular.

His defining moment came at the Beijing 2022 Winter Olympics, when he soared to victory in the large hill individual event, claiming Gold with two flawless jumps and edging out strong competition from Japan and Germany. It was Norway's first Olympic large hill Gold in 58 years, and Lindvik's leap instantly etched his name into national sporting folklore.

Beyond the Olympics, Lindvik has secured multiple World Cup victories. He's particularly dangerous on large hills, with a personal best of 245.5 meters—one of the longest competitive jumps ever recorded.

The seasons following Beijing have seen him navigate the challenges of injury recovery and fierce competition, but he remains a key member of Norway's ski jumping elite.

He contributed to team medals and consistently places near the top in major events, including the prestigious Four Hills Tournament and the World Ski Flying Championships.

Now 27, Lindvik is focused on one thing: defending his Olympic title. With Norway historically dominant in ski jumping, Lindvik not only carries national expectations but also personal ambition—to become one of the rare jumpers to win multiple Olympic golds in the large hill event.

As the countdown to the Milano–Cortina 2026 Games begins, all eyes will be on the icy launch towers of Italy—and the man from Rælingen who once ruled the skies above Beijing.

DID YOU KNOW?

Did you know Norway has won more Winter Olympic medals than any other country?

GERMANY

Francesco Friedrich (GERMANY)
Bobsleigh. 2-man & 4-man.

Double Olympic Champion (2018, 2022) in both two-man and four-man events. Most successful pilot in IBSF World Championships history.

Francesco Friedrich, hailing from Pirna in Saxony, has defined dominance in Men's Bobsleigh. Initially an athletics prodigy, he switched to bobsledding at age 16—quickly mastering the pilot's role and launching a reign that would reshape the sport's record books.

At the PyeongChang 2018 Winter Olympics, Friedrich made history with a sensational double gold, winning both the two-man (tied with Canada's Kripps/Kopacz) and four-man races. He repeated that rare feat at Beijing 2022, defending both titles and powering Germany to the first Olympic Bobsleigh sweep ever.

His Olympic accolades are matched by World Championship excellence: he has secured a staggering number of World titles—both in two-man and four-man disciplines—making him the most decorated pilot in IBSF history.

In the World Cup circuit, Friedrich has been nearly unbeatable. He has swept overall titles across both disciplines—and the combined ranking—across multiple seasons, reaffirming his sustained excellence.

Heading into Milano–Cortina 2026, Friedrich stands as the indisputable favourite for Olympic gold in both the two-man and four-man events. His unparalleled track record, mental precision, and ability to deliver under pressure mark him as the lodestar of German bobsleigh.

With winter's elite eyes on his next moves, Friedrich isn't just racing to win—he's rewriting the benchmark for what it means to dominate.

Christopher Grotheer (GERMANY)
Skeleton

 Christopher Grotheer stepped onto the international skeleton scene in the early 2010's, debuting in the European Cup in 2010. Through early success as a junior world championship silver medallist and steady progress in the World Cup circuit, he built a foundation of grit and precision.

The defining moment of his career came at the Beijing 2022 Winter Olympics, where he shattered expectations—claiming gold in the men's skeleton and becoming the first German to do so in Olympic history.

That victory uplifted Germany's sliding legacy and placed Grotheer front and centre of the global scene. Grotheer's dominance continued post-Beijing. He captured the overall Skeleton World Cup title in 2022–23, demonstrating consistency across multiple venues.

He continues to perform strongly in subsequent seasons, with multiple World Cup event wins—often setting track records, such as his breakthrough performance in Park City.

In the 2024–25 season, Grotheer continues to shine. He won back-to-back races at the season's onset in PyeongChang, jumping from third to first with top times in both runs. He also claimed victory in Lillehammer, leading an all-German podium and emerging atop the World Cup standings.

As the defending Olympic champion, Grotheer arrives in 2026 among the strongest favourites in the men's skeleton. His blend of speed, precision, and calm under pressure, make him a consistent threat. If he replicates his Olympic success in Italy, he won't just defend his title—he'll solidify his legacy as one of the sport's greats.

Christopher Grotheer isn't just winning races; he's crafting history. From Germany's historic Olympic breakthrough to dominating the World Cup circuit, he remains the defining figure of modern skeleton racing. He made history by winning Germany's first Olympic Gold in men's skeleton at the 2022 Beijing Games.

DID YOU KNOW?

Did you know the coldest Games were in Lillehammer 1994, with temperatures dipping below -25°C?

Tobias Wendl & Tobias Arlt (GERMANY) Luge Doubles

Olympic Gold Medallists: 2014, 2018, 2022 (Doubles & Team Relay). Most successful male lugers by Olympic golds (six between them).

When Tobias Wendl and Tobias Arlt take their seats atop the sled, they carry the precision, power, and polish of a championship duo. Since forming their partnership, these two athletes, fondly dubbed—*The Two Tobis*—have elevated the sport of doubles luge to an art form.

Their Olympic journey began in Sochi 2014, where they claimed Gold in both the doubles and team relay, delivering a staggering margin of victory and setting a new track record along the way.

Eight years later, at Beijing 2022, they achieved the rare feat of winning three consecutive Olympic doubles gold medals, while also contributing to relay glory and becoming the most decorated German Winter Olympians with six golds between them.

Their dominance extends far beyond the Olympics. The pair has consistently topped the World Cup standings, securing overall doubles titles across multiple seasons and remaining a formidable force on the circuit.

As they cruise toward their fourth Olympic Games together, Wendl and Arlt remain the pair to beat. Their synergy, born from years of shared training, mutual trust, and unmatched chemistry, makes them a perpetual favourite for another Gold. In a sport where harmony and split-second coordination define victory, their flawless runs continue to inspire both teammates and rivals.

Wendl and Arlt aren't just champions—they're history makers. With every glide, they push the boundaries of precision, endurance, and brilliance. Heading into 2026, the world will watch—and wait—for the next chapter in the legendary story of Germany's luge royalty.

Leon Draisaitl (GERMANY) - Ice Hockey Captain of Germany's national men's team for Milano-Cortina 2026

Leon Draisaitl isn't just Germany's greatest-ever ice hockey player—he's one of the best in the world. A towering presence on the ice at 6'2", the Edmonton Oilers' elite forward combines speed, vision, and clinical finishing in a way few can match. Nicknamed the *"German Gretzky"* by fans, Draisaitl is a former NHL Hart Trophy winner (MVP) and Art Ross Trophy winner as the league's top scorer.

While Draisaitl has spent the bulk of his career lighting up rinks in North America, his heart beats for Germany. The 2026 Winter Olympics in Milano-Cortina mark a major shift. NHL players are once again eligible to compete in Olympic ice hockey. For Germany, that means a massive boost—not just in talent, but in belief.

Draisaitl's return to the international stage rekindles memories of Germany's Cinderella run to silver in PyeongChang 2018—achieved without any NHL stars. Now, with Draisaitl at the centre, the team is no longer a dark horse—it's a powerhouse in the making.

Born in Cologne in 1995, Draisaitl was practically raised in the rink. His father, Peter Draisaitl, was a national team player and coach. Leon's rise was meteoric, and by age 24, he became the first German to lead the NHL in scoring.

With Draisaitl's unmatched hockey IQ, pinpoint passes, and sniper's shot, Germany's men's ice hockey squad heads into 2026 with more firepower than ever before. If they go all the way, it would be one of the greatest stories in Winter Olympic hockey history—and Leon Draisaitl would be its golden centrepiece.

Leon Draisaitl, a star forward for the Edmonton Oilers, leads Germany's ice hockey team. With the return of NHL players to the Olympics, his participation significantly boosts Germany's chances for a historic Gold in men's ice hockey.

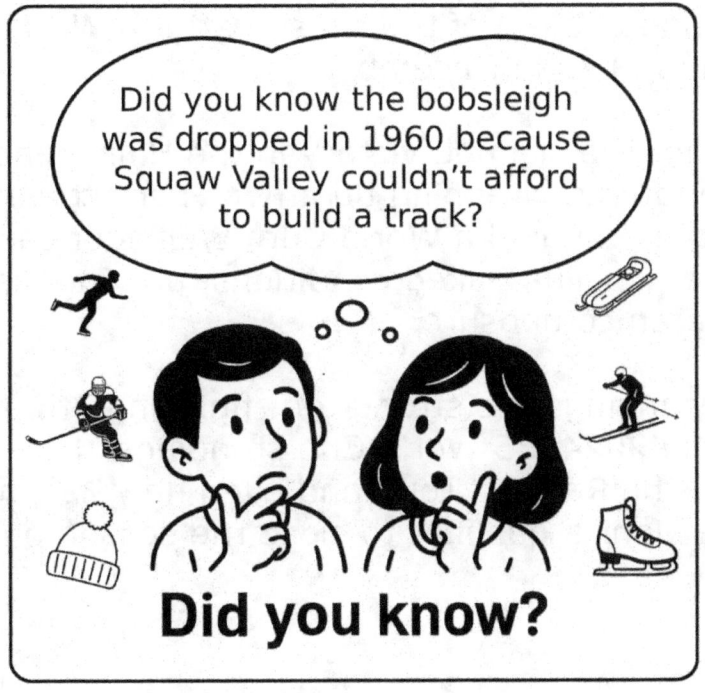

Andreas Wellinger (GERMANY) Ski Jumper

At just 22, Andreas Wellinger soared into history by clinching Germany's first individual Olympic ski jumping Gold since Jens Weißflog's 1994 triumph. His dual medals in 2018 underlined his dominance across both hills.

But glory was interrupted. Wellinger suffered a torn ACL in 2019, alongside other injuries that sidelined him from competition. Yet he fought back with resilience.

His return has been impressive. In Vikersund (2025), he triumphed on the flying hill—his second podium of the season after a World Cup win in Ruka in December.

Earlier, he claimed victory in the Hinzenbach Grand Prix, wrapping up a near-perfect weekend. At the Trondheim World Cup, Wellinger captured silver in rain-soaked conditions, proving his veteran composure.

His rankings are strong too: finishing 7th overall in the 2024–25 World Cup standings. He also won the Raw Air Tour and even flew 227 meters in a Planica qualifier to close the season on a high note.

At 30, Andreas Wellinger is channelling experience and grit into his finest form. With consistent podium finishes and championship wins under his belt, he's poised to challenge—and perhaps reclaim—the Olympic glory he first tasted in 2018.

Andreas Wellinger, boasts this form guide, 2018 Olympic Gold (Normal Hill)—first German to win individual Olympic gold since 1994. Olympic Silver (Large Hill & Team, 2018) & Team Gold (2014). World Championship Silver (2023, 2025); Mixed Team Gold (2017, 2023).

Andreas has remained a strong competitor in ski jumping. With recent podium finishes, he is a serious contender for Gold in 2026.

Jessica Degenhardt & Cheyenne Rosenthal (GERMANY) Women's Doubles Luge

In the world of high-speed ice racing, few pairings have made an impression as quickly—or as dominantly—as Germany's Jessica Degenhardt and Cheyenne Rosenthal. This fearless duo has surged to the forefront of women's doubles luge; a discipline only officially added to the Olympic program in Beijing 2022. As the sport continues to grow, Degenhardt and Rosenthal are poised to make history at Milano-Cortina 2026.

Jessica Degenhardt, born in 2002 in Dresden, was a junior world champion before teaming up with Rosenthal in the senior circuit. Cheyenne Rosenthal, born in 2000 in Winterberg, was herself a European Youth Olympic champion and one of Germany's most promising singles lugers before shifting focus to doubles. Together, they form a partnership that blends fearlessness with finesse.

The two burst onto the senior scene with strong World Cup performances, quickly collecting podiums and wins. During the 2023–24 and 2024–25 seasons, they solidified their position among the world's elite, often battling for top honours with Austrian and Italian rivals. Their chemistry on the sled is unmistakable—precision steering, synchronized movements, and ice-cold nerves through hair-raising turns are now their signature.

Germany has long been the dominant force in Luge. But what sets Degenhardt and Rosenthal apart is their ability to innovate—refining aerodynamic technique, mastering equipment setups, and constantly improving starts. Their consistency on the international stage has made them not just medal favourites, but likely standard-bearers for women's luge in the coming decade.

CANADA

Mikaël Kingsbury (CANADA)
Freestyle Skiing Moguls & Dual Moguls

No one in the history of freestyle skiing has dominated moguls like Mikaël Kingsbury. Known globally as the *"King of Moguls"* Kingsbury's brilliance lies not only in his record-shattering stats but in his relentless pursuit of perfection on the bumps and aerials of his sport.

Since bursting onto the international scene as an 18-year-old in 2010, Kingsbury has rewritten the record books. Heading into Milano-Cortina 2026, he boasts an astonishing 99 World Cup victories, 142 World Cup podiums, and a staggering 29 Crystal Globes—including an unprecedented nine straight overall titles from 2011–2020. He also holds the record for most World Championship podiums and titles in freestyle skiing history.

A three-time Olympic medallist—silver in Sochi 2014, Gold in PyeongChang 2018, and silver again in Beijing 2022—Kingsbury became the first male Moguls skier to reach the Olympic podium three times. With dual moguls added to the Olympic program in 2026, the Canadian has a new opportunity to double his medal count and etch his name even deeper into Olympic lore.

Kingsbury has reached the podium in 15 of 16 starts at the FIS World Championships and gone unbeaten in stretches that seemed impossible, like his 13-event winning streak from 2017–2018.

Despite a serious back injury in 2020 that sidelined him for months, Kingsbury returned to win double Gold at the 2021 World Championships—proof of his grit and greatness.

Off the slopes, Kingsbury is a proud father (welcoming son Henrik in 2024), a golf and hockey enthusiast, and a man who never let go of a childhood dream. At 10, he taped the Olympic rings over his bed with the words: "I will win." He kept that promise—and then some.

As Milano-Cortina 2026 approaches, Mikaël Kingsbury isn't just chasing medals. He's chasing immortality.

Connor McDavid (CANADA)
Ice Hockey Men's Team

Few names in the modern era of ice hockey carry as much weight as Connor McDavid. Dubbed the fastest player on ice and often compared to legends like Wayne Gretzky and Sidney Crosby, McDavid has redefined excellence in the NHL with his unmatched speed, vision, and scoring ability.

Since being selected first overall in the 2015 NHL Draft by the Edmonton Oilers, McDavid has risen to become the league's most electrifying player. He's captured three Hart Trophies as the NHL's Most Valuable Player, and five Art Ross Trophies as the league's top scorer. Under his captaincy, the Oilers have returned to playoff prominence, with McDavid's combination of leadership and explosive play becoming must-watch television.

Now, for the first time in his illustrious career, McDavid will represent Team Canada at the Olympic Games in Milano-Cortina 2026—a moment Canadian hockey fans have long awaited. With the return of NHL players to the Winter Olympics, Canada is poised to ice one of the most talent-laden rosters in history, and McDavid is expected to lead the charge.

He joins a rich lineage of Canadian hockey icons who have worn the maple leaf on the sport's grandest stage.

While he already has a World Championship gold (2016) and a World Cup of Hockey title (2016), the Olympic Gold is the one major accolade that has eluded him—until now.

For McDavid, this Olympic debut is about more than individual glory. It's about fulfilling a lifelong dream and inspiring the next generation of Canadian athletes. With his prime years aligning perfectly with the 2026 Games, Connor McDavid is not just arriving in Italy to compete—he's coming to conquer.

Alexandria Loutitt
Ski Jumping (CANADA)

First Canadian woman to win a World Cup ski jumping event. 2023 World Champion – Large Hill. 2022 Olympic Bronze – Mixed Team Event (Canada's first ski jumping medal).

At just 21 years old, Alexandria Loutitt has already flown into the history books as one of Canada's greatest winter sports trailblazers. In a discipline long dominated by European powerhouses, Loutitt has shattered barriers and rewritten the narrative of Canadian ski jumping.

Loutitt first caught the world's attention at the 2022 Winter Olympics in Beijing, helping Canada earn a surprise bronze medal in the mixed team event—the nation's first Olympic medal in ski jumping. But that was only the beginning.

In 2023, she stunned the ski jumping world by winning the World Championship gold in the large hill—becoming the first Canadian woman to ever capture a world title in the sport. That same year, she also made history on the World Cup circuit, becoming the first Canadian woman to win a World Cup event, claiming Gold in Zao, Japan.

Loutitt's rise is more than athletic achievement; it's a story of resilience and belief.

Growing up in Calgary, Alberta, she began jumping at the iconic Canada Olympic Park. But as Canada's ski jumping infrastructure declined, she moved overseas as a teenager to train in Europe, sacrificing proximity to family for the chance to compete on the world stage. Her decision has paid off spectacularly.

Now, with the 2026 Milano-Cortina Olympics on the horizon, Loutitt isn't just a medal hopeful—she's a favourite...and why wouldn't she be with this form guide?

She is the first Canadian woman ever to win a World Cup ski jumping event. In 2023 Loutitt was crowned World Champion (Large Hill) — Canada's first world title in ski jumping.

Her technical precision, quiet confidence, and relentless drive have positioned her to possibly secure Canada's first-ever Olympic Gold in ski jumping.

Deanna Stellato-Dudek & Maxime Deschamps (CANADA) Figure Skating Pairs

Deanna Stellato-Dudek and Maxime Deschamps are not just skating for Gold—they're skating for the history books. They were 2024 World Champions and three-time Canadian National Champions.

In 2024, the Canadian duo shocked the figure skating world by capturing the World Championship title in pairs skating. For Deschamps, a steady presence in Canada's skating scene, it was a crowning achievement. For Stellato-Dudek, it was nothing short of extraordinary: At age 41, she became the oldest woman to ever win a World Championship in figure skating.

Stellato-Dudek's story is the stuff of legend. A promising American singles skater in the late 1990s, she won silver at the 2000 World Junior Championships before retiring at just 17 due to injury. For over 15 years, she stepped away from the sport—until an almost unthinkable comeback began.

In her 30s, Stellato-Dudek returned to competitive skating—not in singles, but in pairs—and later switched nationalities to represent Canada alongside Deschamps. The pair quickly built momentum, winning their first Canadian title in 2022 and steadily climbing the international ranks.

Their journey has been marked by resilience, chemistry, and precision. Their programs combine powerful lifts with emotional storytelling, capturing audiences and judges alike. At the 2024 World Championships, they delivered two near-flawless performances, standing atop the podium against much younger competition.

As the 2026 Milano-Cortina Olympics approach, Stellato-Dudek and Deschamps are among the top contenders for Olympic gold. Their partnership is a symbol of passion, perseverance, and the belief that greatness knows no age limit.

For fans of Olympic sport, theirs is a tale that resonates far beyond the rink—a story of second chances, enduring dreams, and the artistry of skating that spans generations. Should they triumph in Italy, it would be one of the most inspiring chapters in Winter Olympic history.

Reece Howden – (CANADA)
Freestyle Skiing Ski Cross

In the adrenaline-fueled world of ski cross, where speed, precision, and fearlessness collide, Reece Howden has carved out a reputation as one of the sport's most formidable competitors. With three Crystal Globes to his name and 18 World Cup victories, the 26-year-old Canadian is primed to chase Olympic glory at the Milano-Cortina 2026 Winter Games.

Born in Chilliwack, British Columbia, Howden grew up skiing the snowy slopes of western Canada, quickly transitioning from alpine skiing to ski cross—where multiple racers launch out of the start gate and fly down a twisting, jump-laden course side by side. The physical and mental demands are intense, but Howden thrives under pressure.

He made his World Cup debut in 2018, and by the 2020–21 season, he had exploded onto the scene with dominance rarely seen in ski cross. That year, he won five races, clinching his first Crystal Globe as the overall World Cup champion. Since then, he has consistently remained at the top, demonstrating remarkable consistency, raw speed, and tactical brilliance.

Despite narrowly missing the podium at the Beijing 2022 Winter Olympics, Howden's resilience has only grown. In recent seasons, he has sharpened his starts, refined his passing strategy, and continued stacking up wins against the best in the world. His performances on the World Cup circuit have marked him as one of the favourites heading into Milano-Cortina.

What sets Howden apart is not only his athleticism but his analytical mind. He studies each course meticulously and adjusts his race plan with precision. Off the hill, he is known for his calm demeanour and leadership within the Canadian ski cross team.

As the 2026 Games approach, Canada's hopes in ski cross will ride heavily on Reece Howden's shoulders. With unmatched momentum and a hunger to finally stand on the Olympic podium, he is more than just a contender—he is a true medal threat.

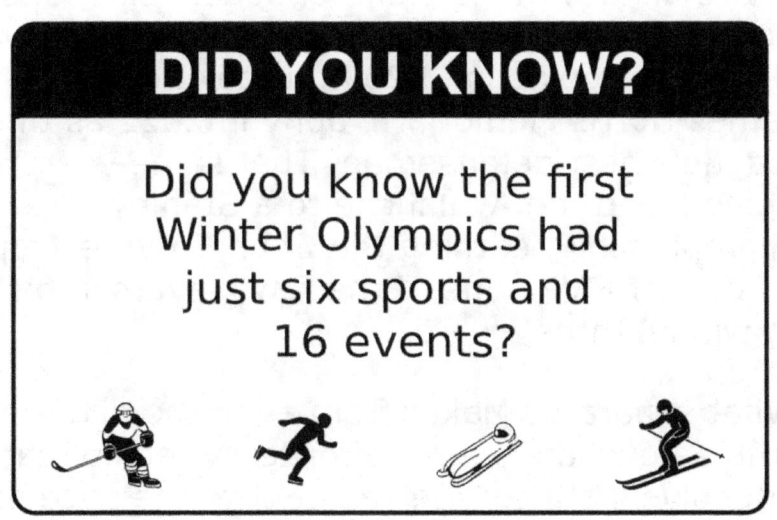

DID YOU KNOW?

Did you know the first Winter Olympics had just six sports and 16 events?

Cale Makar (CANADA)
Ice Hockey Men's Team

At just 26 years old, Cale Makar has already rewritten the playbook for what a modern NHL defenseman can be. A generational talent with an almost balletic skating stride, Makar is widely considered one of the best—and most exciting—blue-liners in the world.

With the return of NHL players to the Olympic stage, Makar is poised to make his Olympic debut at Milano-Cortina 2026, and he's expected to play a pivotal role in Team Canada's pursuit of Gold.

Born in Calgary, Alberta, Makar was selected 4th overall by the Colorado Avalanche in the 2017 NHL Draft. Since then, he has dazzled fans and critics alike with his blend of speed, skill, and hockey IQ. He won the Calder Trophy as the NHL's top rookie in 2020 and took home the James Norris Memorial Trophy in 2022 as the league's best defenseman. That same year, he helped lead the Avalanche to a Stanley Cup championship, earning the Conn Smythe Trophy as playoff MVP—one of the few players in history to win all three awards.

What separates Makar from even the elite tier of NHL defensemen is his effortless mobility and offensive instincts. He can control the pace of a game from the back end, quarterback a power play with precision, and shut down the opposition's top forwards with poise.

For Canada, Makar brings the total package: elite two-way play, big-game experience, and the calm confidence of a champion. On Olympic ice—wider and faster—his skating will be an even greater asset. With Connor McDavid and Sidney Crosby likely joining him on the roster, Canada is assembling a dream team of talent, and Makar is a central piece of that puzzle.

As he suits up in the red and white for the first time on Olympic ice, Cale Makar is not just a player to watch—he's a player to build around. And for Canadian fans, he may be the key to reclaiming hockey supremacy on the world's biggest stage.

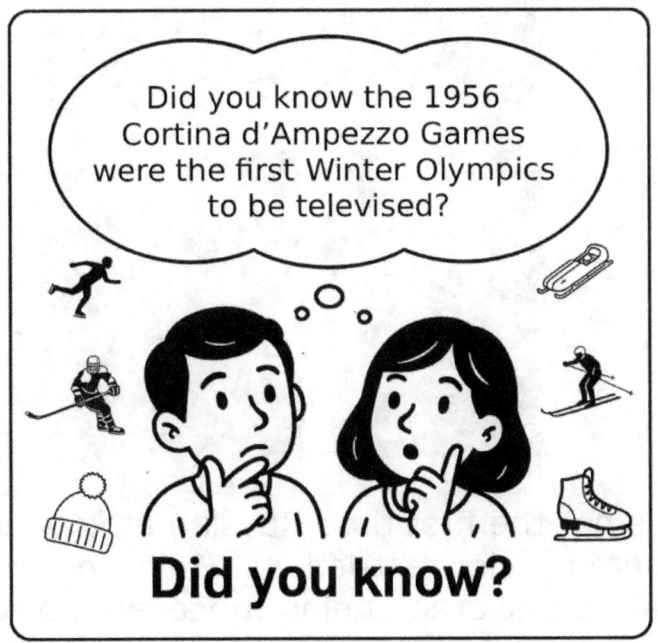

Did you know the 1956 Cortina d'Ampezzo Games were the first Winter Olympics to be televised?

Did you know?

About RUSSIA and Individual Neutral Athletes (AIN)

The upcoming Milan-Cortina 2026 Winter Olympics will once again highlight the intersection of sport and geopolitics, as Russian athletes face restrictions stemming from the nation's 2022 invasion of Ukraine.

The International Olympic Committee (IOC) has maintained its March 2023 recommendation that Russian and Belarusian athletes may not compete as National teams. Instead, a limited number may be allowed to participate only as Individual Neutral Athletes (INA)—a designation that bars national symbols, flags, anthems, and collective representation.

This is not the first time Russian athletes have competed under restrictions. Following revelations of state-sponsored doping, uncovered after the

2014 Sochi Games, Russia was suspended from Olympic competition beginning in 2017.

At PyeongChang 2018, Russian athletes competed as "Olympic Athletes from Russia" (OAR). They were subject to strict neutrality requirements, including competing under the Olympic flag. Similar rules applied at Tokyo 2020 and Beijing 2022, where Russian athletes entered under the banner of the "Russian Olympic Committee."

The 2026 sanctions differ in both tone and scope. While previous bans centred on doping violations, the current measures are a direct response to geopolitical aggression. The IOC and numerous international federations determined that Russia's invasion of Ukraine created an environment of unfairness and potential safety risks for Ukrainian athletes. Consequently, Russian teams, such as men's and women's ice hockey squads, will remain completely excluded in Milan.

Individual participation is possible, but only under tight conditions. Athletes must undergo a rigorous vetting process to ensure they have no active ties to the Russian military or national security apparatus. Each case is reviewed by international sports federations, with final approval resting with the IOC. Those cleared to compete will do so in plain uniforms devoid of National insignia. Medal ceremonies will feature the Olympic anthem, not Russia's.

Adelia Petrosian (AIN)
Figure Skating Women's Singles

At just 18 years old, Adelia Petrosian is already redefining the limits of what's possible in women's figure skating. Known for her daring technical arsenal—including multiple quadruple jumps—Petrosian has become one of the most electrifying and promising young talents on the global skating stage.

Born in Moscow in 2007, Petrosian burst into the spotlight by winning the 2022 Russian National Championship, dazzling audiences with her fearless approach to choreography and her flawless execution of high-difficulty elements. She became the first female skater to land a quadruple loop in competition, a jump so difficult that even seasoned male skaters rarely attempt it.

While political and eligibility issues had kept Russian athletes out of recent international competitions, Petrosian has now been cleared to compete at the 2026 Milano-Cortina Winter Olympics as an Individual Neutral Athlete (AIN).

Despite not skating under the Russian flag, she is poised to make a statement that transcends nationality.

What sets Petrosian apart isn't just her quads—it's her balance of artistry and athleticism. Under the tutelage of renowned coach Eteri Tutberidze, she blends cutting-edge technique with emotive musical interpretation, making her performances as memorable artistically as they are technically astonishing.

As she prepares for her Olympic debut, expectations are sky-high. She will face fierce competition from Japanese, South Korean, and American skaters, many of whom have also pushed the technical envelope in recent years.

But Petrosian's fearless mindset and competitive consistency make her one of the most dangerous contenders for gold. More than just a prodigy, Adelia Petrosian represents the future of women's figure skating—a future where athleticism and elegance coexist, and where the impossible is made routine.

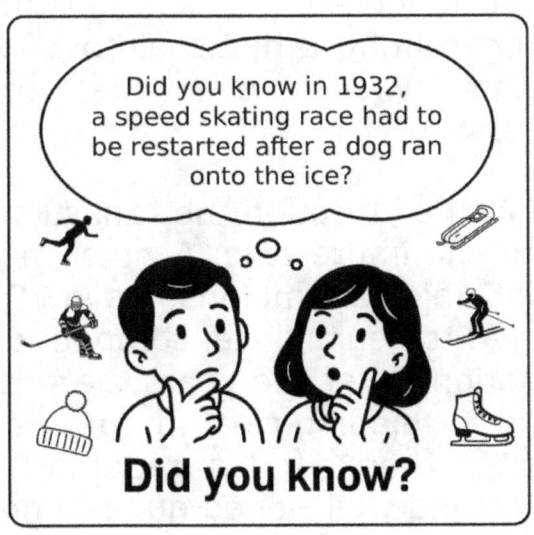

Petr Gumennik (AIN)
Figure Skating Men's Singles

In the often-unpredictable world of figure skating, consistency is a rare and valuable commodity. Petr Gumennik, a 22-year-old figure skater from Russia, embodies this elusive quality—blending rock-solid technique with elegant artistry to emerge as one of the brightest talents heading into the 2026 Winter Olympics in Milano-Cortina.

Representing Russia as an Individual Neutral Athlete (INA) due to ongoing international regulations, Gumennik enters the Olympic spotlight with serious momentum. He recently claimed victory at the 2025 Russian Grand Prix Final, delivering back-to-back performances that showcased his blend of emotional interpretation and technical finesse. His skating is poetic without being overwrought, athletic without being rigid—a balance that few achieve and even fewer sustain under pressure.

Gumennik's rise through the ranks has been deliberate and impressive. A silver medallist at the World Junior Championships in 2019, he's transitioned to senior-level competition with quiet determination. Over the years, he's built a reputation for landing clean programs while others falter, thanks to his trademark calm composure and well-honed quad jumps.

What sets Gumennik apart is not just his technical skill, but his storytelling on the ice. His programs are carefully crafted to connect with audiences and judges alike, bringing a sense of depth and maturity to his performances. It's no wonder he's been praised for being *"an old soul in young skates."*

Now, with the 2026 Olympics looming, Gumennik is more than just a dark horse—he's a genuine medal contender. With many top skaters facing injuries or inconsistency, his stability and artistry could be his greatest weapons in a high-stakes field.

Though he may not wear the Russian flag on his costume, Petr Gumennik carries with him the hopes of fans who admire resilience, elegance, and the quiet determination it takes to rise in a fiercely competitive sport.

DID YOU KNOW?

Did you know the 1964 Innsbruck Olympics had to fly in snow by helicopter because of a freak thaw?

Alexander Bolshunov (AIN)
Cross-Country Skiing

Few athletes in the history of cross-country skiing have combined power, precision, and endurance quite like Alexander Bolshunov. The Russian skiing powerhouse has already etched his name into Olympic history, and as the 2026 Winter Games in Milano-Cortina approach, he remains one of the most feared competitors on snow.

Bolshunov's career achievements are staggering. A three-time Olympic Gold medallist, he triumphed at the Beijing 2022 Games in dominant fashion—claiming victory in the skiathlon, the 50km freestyle, and the 4x10km relay. Alongside his golds, he has also amassed multiple silver and bronze medals, proving his versatility across distances and techniques. In the World Cup circuit, Bolshunov has twice claimed the coveted overall crystal globe, underlining his status as a season-long competitor, not just a championship performer.

What makes Bolshunov extraordinary is his combination of raw strength and impeccable technique. His relentless pace over long distances can shatter the will of opponents, while his smooth, efficient style allows him to conserve energy and finish with devastating sprints. He is equally dangerous in classic and freestyle disciplines, a versatility that keeps rivals guessing and often powerless.

Born in Podyvotye, Bryansk Oblast, Bolshunov rose through Russia's development system with remarkable speed. By his early 20s, he was already winning medals at the highest level. His competitive drive has occasionally sparked headlines, as he races with an intensity that brooks no compromise—whether in a sprint duel or a punishing 50km grind.

Heading into Milano-Cortina 2026, Bolshunov will compete under the status of an Individual Neutral Athlete due to international regulations. Even without the Russian flag on his uniform, his presence will command attention.

Alexandra Trusova (AIN)
Figure Skating Women's Singles

Few figure skaters in history have redefined the boundaries of technical possibility quite like Alexandra Trusova. Dubbed the "Quad Queen", she is the first woman to land five quadruple jumps in a single program, an achievement that not only stunned the figure skating world but also cemented her as a revolutionary force in the sport.

Trusova's international career took flight early. Bursting onto the scene as a junior, she was the first female skater to land a quad toe loop, quad lutz, and quad flip in competition. Her fearless approach to pushing technical limits quickly earned her a reputation as one of the sport's boldest innovators.

At the Beijing 2022 Winter Olympics, she delivered a historic free skate that included five quads, earning the silver medal and narrowly missing the top podium spot. That performance remains one of the most talked-about moments in Olympic figure skating history.

While her jumps have garnered headlines, Trusova has also worked to refine her artistry and skating skills, balancing her explosive technical arsenal with improved choreography and presentation. Her combination of athletic power and increasing artistic maturity makes her a rare all-around threat in a discipline often divided between jump specialists and performance-oriented skaters.

The road to Milano-Cortina 2026 is not without uncertainty. As a Russian athlete, Trusova's participation depends on eligibility rulings and her approval to compete as an Individual Neutral Athlete. If cleared, she will arrive as one of the most dangerous contenders in the women's field. Few, if any, rivals can match her technical content when she delivers at her best.

Off the ice, Trusova is admired for her determination, resilience, and willingness to challenge conventions. Her drive to achieve what others deemed impossible has inspired a new generation of young skaters to dream bigger and attempt more daring elements.

DID YOU KNOW?

Did you know curling was featured in 1924 but then disappeared until 1998?

Anastasia Mishina & Aleksandr Galliamov (AIN) Figure Skating

Anastasia Mishina and Aleksandr Galliamov have rapidly established themselves among the elite in pairs figure skating, combining flawless synchronization with exceptional technical difficulty.

Representing Russia, the duo captured Olympic bronze at Beijing 2022 and were crowned World Champions in 2021, showcasing a blend of power, artistry, and unshakable competitive composure.

Their rise has been meteoric. Mishina, known for her elegance and remarkable consistency, and Galliamov, admired for his explosive lifts and strong presence, first joined forces in 2017. From the start, their partnership clicked—winning the World Junior Championship in 2019 and transitioning seamlessly to senior competition.

Within just two seasons on the senior stage, they were dominating major events, defeating seasoned veterans and pushing the sport's technical boundaries.

At the 2021 World Championships in Stockholm, Mishina and Galliamov delivered two stunning programs to claim the gold medal in their debut appearance at the event. Their precision in side-by-side jumps, seamless throws, and unison in spins set them apart from the competition. The following year, at the Beijing Olympics, they overcame immense pressure to stand on the podium with bronze—an impressive achievement for such a young team on sport's grandest stage.

Heading toward the Milano-Cortina 2026 Winter Olympics, their ambitions are set higher. They are working to refine their artistry to match their technical prowess, aiming to deliver programs that both wow the judges and resonate emotionally with audiences. Known for difficult elements like throw triple flips and side-by-side triple salchows, they consistently push themselves to elevate their technical base value.

Mishina and Galliamov's journey is defined by discipline, trust, and a relentless drive to improve. If given the chance, they could write the next golden chapter in their remarkable career.

DID YOU KNOW?

Did you know in the 1960 Games, Walt Disney helped plan the opening ceremony, including a 5,000-person choir?

Kamila Valieva (AIN)
Figure Skating (Women's Singles)

Kamila Valieva burst onto the international figure skating scene as one of the most gifted talents of her generation, blending extraordinary technical difficulty with unmatched artistic expression.

At just 15, she captured the 2022 European Championship title, delivering performances that combined elegance, fluidity, and the rare ability to land multiple quadruple jumps—a feat few women in history have accomplished.

Valieva's skating is marked by her seamless transitions, musical interpretation, and balletic movement. Off the ice, she is softly spoken and disciplined, but on the ice, she transforms into a commanding performer capable of captivating global audiences.

Her breakout senior season in 2021–22 saw her win the Grand Prix Final, multiple Grand Prix events, and Russian National Championships, establishing her as the Olympic favourite heading into Beijing 2022. However, her Olympic debut became overshadowed by a highly publicized doping controversy that emerged during the Games.

Although she was allowed to compete in the women's singles event, the intense media scrutiny and emotional strain saw her falter in the free skate, finishing fourth despite a strong short program. The situation left the figure skating world divided and sparked debate over athlete welfare, anti-doping processes, and the pressures placed on young competitors.

Since then, Valieva's eligibility for future competitions has been under question, with her participation in the Milano-Cortina 2026 Winter Olympics dependent on formal clearance. If allowed to compete, she would return to the Olympic stage with a chance to redeem her unfinished story—this time as a more mature, experienced athlete.

Her technical arsenal remains formidable. She is among the few women capable of performing both triple axels and quadruple jumps in competition while maintaining world-class artistry. Valieva's career is already one of the most talked-about in modern figure skating.

Note: On the following pages we showcase outstanding athletes from nations beyond the USA, Canada, Russia, Norway, and Germany—countries long regarded as powerhouses of winter sport. Whilst some of the following competitors are definite medal prospects, the Trailblazers bring talent, determination, and the spirit of possibility to the Milano-Cortina Winter Olympics.

Ester Ledecká (CZECH REPUBLIC) Super-G alpine skiing & snowboard parallel giant slalom

When the world gathers in Italy for the 2026 Winter Olympics in Milano-Cortina, few athletes will command as much attention as Ester Ledecká of the Czech Republic. A trailblazer in every sense, Ledecká has already etched her name into Olympic history by becoming the only woman to win Gold in two different sports at the same Winter Games.

At PyeongChang 2018, she stunned the sporting world by winning the Super-G alpine skiing title just days before claiming gold in the snowboard parallel giant slalom. Four years later in Beijing 2022, she successfully defended her snowboard crown, cementing her place among the all-time greats. Her ability to master two technically demanding disciplines remains virtually unmatched in Olympic competition.

Now, heading into 2026, Ledecká is once again a headline act. Recently crowned 2025 World Champion in parallel giant slalom, she shows no sign of slowing down. Her trademark versatility, switching seamlessly from skis to snowboard, makes her both a fan favourite and a nightmare for rivals.

Preparation for Milano-Cortina has been intense. The Czech star has balanced training camps across Europe, fine-tuning her speed and precision. While most athletes devote entire careers to mastering one event, Ledecká continues to chase perfection in two. Her fearless style, combined with her tactical intelligence, ensures she remains a genuine contender in both alpine skiing and snowboarding.

"I've never wanted to choose between skiing and snowboarding—I love them both too much. The Olympics are where I prove that it's possible to do both."

Ester Ledecká

Zoi Sadowski-Synnott (NZ) Slopestyle & Big Air

When Zoi Sadowski-Synnott takes to the slopes at the 2026 Winter Olympics in Milano-Cortina, she will do so carrying the hopes of an entire nation. Already New Zealand's most successful winter athlete, Sadowski-Synnott has transformed her country into a force on the snowboarding stage.

Her breakthrough came at the PyeongChang 2018 Games, when she captured bronze in big air at just 16 years old—New Zealand's first Olympic medal in snow sports. But it was at the Beijing 2022 Olympics that she truly made history.

With breathtaking skill and fearless execution, she claimed Gold in Slopestyle and silver in big air, instantly becoming a national icon and cementing her place among snowboarding's global elite.

Since then, Sadowski-Synnott has only grown stronger. She has amassed multiple X Games Gold medals and World Championship titles, proving her ability to perform under pressure against the best in the world. Known for her smooth style and progressive tricks—often pushing the boundaries of what women's snowboarding can achieve—she has redefined the sport for a new generation.

Now, as she prepares for Milano-Cortina 2026, Sadowski-Synnott is determined to build on her legacy. Training across New Zealand, Europe, and North America, she continues to refine her runs, adding new technical elements and innovative spins. At just 25, she combines the fearlessness of youth with the experience of a seasoned champion, making her one of the favourites for slopestyle and big air once again.

Her impact extends far beyond medals. Zoi has become a role model for young athletes across New Zealand, inspiring a new wave of snowboarders to chase big dreams. She has also played a pivotal role in raising the profile of snowboarding in Oceania, a region better known for surfing and rugby.

"When I'm out there, it's all about pushing limits. That's where the magic happens."

Zoi Sadowski-Synnott

Trailblazers- Mica Moore: Making history with Jamaica Bobsleigh squad

Mica Moore's sporting journey is as remarkable as it is unconventional. A former Welsh sprinter turned bobsledder; Moore is now preparing to write a new chapter of Olympic history as she sets her sights on representing Jamaica at the 2026 Winter Olympics in Milano-Cortina.

Moore first burst onto the international scene as part of Team GB's bobsleigh squad, competing at the 2018 Winter Olympics in PyeongChang. Her explosive sprinting background—she once represented Wales at the Commonwealth Games—made her a natural fit as a brake woman. While she enjoyed success, including top 10 World Cup finishes, funding challenges and team selection issues forced her to rethink her future in the sport.

That turning point sparked an extraordinary shift. Embracing her Jamaican heritage, Moore began working with the Jamaican bobsleigh program, the same program that captured the world's imagination in 1988 and inspired the beloved film *Cool Runnings*. With Jamaica eager to build depth and competitiveness in women's bobsleigh, Moore's experience and athleticism provided the perfect boost.

Now, as she trains towards Milano-Cortina 2026, Moore is blending her sprint speed, Olympic experience, and newfound determination to push Jamaican bobsleigh into uncharted territory. If she qualifies, she will become one of the rare athletes to represent two different nations in Winter Olympic competition—a testament to her resilience and adaptability.

At 33, Moore is at her athletic peak, combining power and wisdom. As she prepares to slide into history, she embodies both the pioneering spirit of Jamaican bobsleigh and the determination of an athlete unwilling to give up on her Olympic dreams.

"It's about proving to myself—and to others—that with resilience and belief, barriers can be broken."

Mica Moore

DID YOU KNOW?

Did you know ice hockey pucks must be frozen before games to reduce bouncing?

Brogan Crowley, Matt Weston & Marcus Wyatt (GB) – Skeleton athletes

Great Britain has long been a powerhouse in skeleton racing, and the upcoming 2026 Winter Olympics in Milano-Cortina promises to showcase another chapter in this proud tradition. Leading the charge are Brogan Crowley, Matt Weston, and Marcus Wyatt—three athletes who are not only carrying Britain's legacy but also setting new standards in the sport.

Brogan Crowley has emerged as one of the strongest women in the international skeleton circuit. A former heptathlete, she switched to skeleton and quickly rose through the ranks, demonstrating both speed and technical mastery. Crowley has delivered consistent World Cup results and is widely seen as a strong contender to follow in the footsteps of British Olympic medallists like Amy Williams and Lizzy Yarnold. Her explosive starts and fearless runs mark her as one of Britain's brightest medals hope in Italy.

Matt Weston has already made history for Team GB, becoming the first British man to win a Skeleton World Championship Gold in 2023. Known for his powerful push starts and unflinching precision on the ice, Weston has consistently been at the sharp end of World Cup standings. His breakthrough season included multiple podiums and cemented his status as one of the world's elite sliders. As Britain looks ahead to Milan, Weston is firmly in the conversation as a gold-medal favourite.

Alongside Weston is teammate Marcus Wyatt, whose resilience and consistency have kept Britain among the best. Wyatt has secured multiple top 10 finishes on the World Cup circuit, with podium highlights proving his ability to challenge the sport's traditional powerhouses. His partnership with Weston has created a formidable British presence in men's skeleton, giving Team GB unprecedented depth.

Together, Crowley, Weston, and Wyatt represent a new golden generation for British skeleton. With Weston's proven championship pedigree, Crowley's rapid rise, and Wyatt's steady determination, Great Britain enters Milano-Cortina with real medal prospects.

DID YOU KNOW?

Did you know the first Winter Olympics were held in Chamonix, France, in 1924?

Kirsty Muir (GB) Big air & Slopestyle

At just 21 years old, Kirsty Muir has already carved out a reputation as one of Great Britain's brightest winter sports stars. Hailing from Aberdeen, Scotland, Muir has been a standout in freestyle skiing, particularly in big air and slopestyle, disciplines that demand equal measures of courage, creativity, and technical mastery.

Muir's Olympic journey began at Beijing 2022, where, as a teenager, she impressed the world by reaching the final of the big air competition and finishing fifth overall—an extraordinary achievement for her debut Games. Competing against the most seasoned freestyle skiers in the world, she displayed both composure and flair, earning praise for her smooth style and willingness to push the limits of difficulty.

Since Beijing, Muir has continued her ascent on the international stage. She has collected multiple World Cup podiums, consistently finishing among the top athletes in big air and slopestyle. Her progression is marked not only by results but also by the innovation she brings to her runs—throwing tricks that only a handful of female skier's attempt. This fearless approach has made her one of the most exciting athletes to watch on the circuit.

Looking ahead to the 2026 Milano-Cortina Winter Olympics, Muir represents a new wave of British freestyle skiers capable of competing with the traditional snow sport powerhouses. With her blend of youthful energy and growing experience, she is poised to challenge for Britain's first-ever Olympic medal in women's freestyle skiing.

What makes Muir particularly compelling is her attitude. Grounded and determined, she often speaks about the joy of progression, the thrill of pushing herself, and inspiring the next generation of young athletes in the UK. She carries not only her own ambitions but also the hopes of a nation eager to see British talent shine in freestyle skiing. As the Games in Italy draw closer, Kirsty Muir will be one to watch.

American Rivers family (JAMAICA) representing Jamaica

History could be written at the 2026 Milano-Cortina Winter Olympics if the Rivers family earns selection to represent Jamaica. Led by Father Henri Rivers, a respected figure in the skiing world, the family's story is both unique and inspiring: a group of talented athletes with Caribbean roots aiming to shine on the slopes of Italy.

Henri Rivers, a seasoned skier and advocate for diversity in winter sports, has raised his children on the mountains since they were young. His triplets—Helaina, Kai, and Max Rivers—have grown up skiing with skill and passion, competing regularly in the United States and Europe. Now, they are turning their eyes toward representing Jamaica, a nation better known for sprinting and, of course, its iconic bobsled team of *Cool Runnings* fame.

The Rivers family recently arrived in Kingston, where they have begun discussions with the Jamaica Olympic Association (JOA). They met with JOA President Christopher Samuda and CEO Ryan Foster to outline their vision.

Among the triplets, Helaina Rivers is already showing promise in slalom and giant slalom, two of the most technically demanding alpine events.

Her fluid turns and aggressive style on the gates have caught attention internationally. Kai and Max, equally determined, are honing their skills in various alpine disciplines, giving Jamaica the prospect of a multi-athlete ski team for the first time in its history.

If selected, the Rivers family would follow in the footsteps of Jamaica's pioneering winter Olympians, bringing fresh energy and a powerful story of representation. Competing under the green, gold, and black, the family could inspire not just Jamaicans, but aspiring athletes from all underrepresented backgrounds in winter sport.

As Milan-Cortina 2026 approaches, the possibility of the Rivers family lining up on the start gates offers a powerful reminder: the Olympic spirit is about more than geography or tradition—it's about passion, perseverance, and breaking boundaries.

DID YOU KNOW?

Did you know the USA hosted the Winter Olympics four times, more than any other country?

Jesper Pedersen (NORWAY) Slalom Sitting

When the world's best Paralympic skiers gather at the 2026 Milano-Cortina Winter Games, few names will command as much respect as Jesper Pedersen of Norway. A master of the slalom sitting discipline, Pedersen has already established himself as one of the most decorated Para alpine skiers of his generation.

Born with spina bifida, Pedersen first took to the slopes as a child and quickly discovered that skiing was not just a sport, but his passion. Over the years, he developed into a technical specialist whose agility, balance, and fearless approach in the sit-ski have set him apart on the world stage.

Pedersen made his Paralympic debut at PyeongChang 2018, where he immediately stamped his authority by winning gold in the giant slalom sitting event, along with several strong finishes across the program. By the time he arrived in Beijing 2022, he was in his prime, and he delivered one of the most dominant performances of the Games—winning four gold medals and one silver, making him Norway's standout star of the Paralympics.

Beyond the Paralympic stage, Pedersen has collected numerous World Championship and World Cup victories, consistently topped standings and pushed the technical limits of the sport. His slalom and giant slalom runs are defined by razor-sharp turns and unflinching confidence.

Looking ahead to Milan-Cortina 2026, Pedersen will be 26 years old—an age considered the peak for many alpine athletes. With his blend of experience, resilience, and an ever-growing trophy cabinet, he enters Italy as the man to beat in slalom sitting.

Norway, a traditional powerhouse in winter sports, will look to him not only for medals but also for inspiration, as he embodies the nation's enduring legacy of excellence on snow.

For Jesper Pedersen, the 2026 Games represent more than just another chance at glory—they are the continuation of a remarkable journey defined by determination, technical mastery, and the pursuit of perfection.

Momoka Muraoka (JAPAN)
Giant Slalom Sitting

Few athletes embody resilience, determination, and excellence on snow quite like Momoka Muraoka, Japan's trailblazing Para alpine skier. At just 27 years old, she has already become one of the most successful Paralympians in her nation's history—and all signs point to her adding even more accolades at the 2026 Winter Paralympic Games in Italy.

Muraoka, who was left paralysed from the waist down due to an illness in childhood, first turned to sport as a way of reclaiming her independence. Her entry into skiing came through Japan's Paralympic development programs, where she quickly discovered a natural aptitude for speed, technical precision, and fierce competitiveness. By her teenage years, she was competing at the international level, laying the foundation for what would become a stellar career.

Her Paralympic breakthrough came at PyeongChang 2018, where she stormed the podium with an astonishing five medals—including a historic gold in the giant slalom sitting event, making her the first Japanese female Winter Paralympian to achieve such a feat. Four years later, at Beijing 2022, she cemented her legacy with another dominant display, capturing three gold medals and a silver, and firmly establishing herself as one of the sport's brightest stars.

Muraoka's skiing is defined by her technical mastery in slalom and giant slalom, as well as her calmness under pressure. She often speaks about the mental side of competition, crediting her success to focus, preparation, and a love for racing at the highest level.

Beyond her personal triumphs, she has become a powerful symbol of representation for disability sport in Japan, inspiring a new generation of athletes to pursue their dreams regardless of barriers.

With her mix of experience, drive, and proven ability to perform when it matters most, she will enter Italy not just as a contender—but as a favourite. For Japan, Momoka Muraoka is more than a Paralympic champion; she is a national icon, poised to once again carry her country's hopes onto the world stage.

Giacomo Bertagnolli (ITALY)
Slalom and Giant Slalom Paralympics

When Italy hosts the 2026 Winter Paralympic Games in Milan-Cortina, one of the brightest hopes for home success will be Giacomo Bertagnolli, the nation's most decorated Para alpine skier.

Born with a visual impairment, Bertagnolli has carved out an extraordinary career on the slopes, combining raw speed, flawless technique, and remarkable resilience to become a global star in his sport.

Bertagnolli burst onto the international scene as a teenager, quickly establishing himself as a force in the visually impaired category, where he races with the help of a sighted guide. His breakthrough came at the 2018 PyeongChang Paralympic Games, where he claimed four medals—including two golds in slalom and giant slalom. At just 19 years old, he became a household name in Italy and a beacon of inspiration for Paralympic sport.

He followed that up with another glittering performance at the Beijing 2022 Paralympic Games, winning two additional gold medals, further cementing his place as one of the finest Para alpine skiers of his generation.

Known for his mastery in the technical disciplines of slalom and giant slalom, Bertagnolli is admired for his smooth coordination with his guide and his ability to deliver under the highest pressure.

Beyond his medal count, Bertagnolli embodies the values of determination and perseverance. His success has raised the profile of Paralympic sport in Italy, inspiring countless young athletes with disabilities to pursue competitive skiing. With Italy set to host the Paralympics for the first time since 2006 (Torino), his presence on home snow carries even greater symbolic weight.

As the countdown to Milan-Cortina 2026 continues, Bertagnolli remains one of Italy's strongest contenders for multiple medals.
For Italian fans, Giacomo Bertagnolli is more than just an athlete—he is a national hero, poised to deliver history on home soil. If his past performances are any indication, the world can expect fireworks when he takes to the snow in 2026.

WINTER OLYMPIC CHAMPIONS

This final section of the book is dedicated to Outstanding Winter Olympians since the Winter Games began in 1924 and Paralympians since the Paralympics began in 1976.

The Paralympic movement was born after World War II when Dr. Ludwig Guttmann, a German-born British neurologist, began using sport to help rehabilitate injured soldiers. His efforts led to the first Stoke Mandeville Games in 1948 for athletes with spinal cord injuries — the foundation of the Paralympic movement.

The first Winter Paralympics were in 1976. These inaugural Winter Paralympic Games were held in Örnsköldsvik, Sweden, with around 250 athletes from 16 countries. There were only two sports: Alpine skiing and Cross-country skiing. Most competitors were amputees or visually impaired athletes, using specially adapted equipment.

Marit Bjørgen – The Queen of the Winter Olympics

Norway's Marit Bjørgen is universally hailed as *the most decorated Winter Olympian of all time.*

Between 2002 and 2018, this cross-country skiing powerhouse amassed 15 Olympic medals — including eight golds, four silvers, and three bronzes — across five consecutive Games. Her success elevated her beyond national hero status to become a symbol of endurance, versatility, and humility in sport.

Born in 1980 in Rognes, Norway, Bjørgen grew up surrounded by snow and the Nordic culture of skiing. She joined the Norwegian national team in 1999 and first made her Olympic debut at Salt Lake City 2002. After an early bronze, her real dominance began in Vancouver 2010, where she captured three gold medals, a silver, and a bronze — a performance that cemented her as the "Queen of the Trails." She continued to reign supreme at Sochi 2014, claiming another three golds, and capped her career with two more medals in PyeongChang 2018 before retiring. What set Bjørgen apart was not only her strength and stamina but her adaptability. She mastered both sprint and long-distance events, an almost impossible feat in cross-country skiing. Her fierce rivalry and friendship with fellow Norwegians like Therese Johaug pushed her to new heights. Off the snow, Bjørgen became a national role model, advocating for equal recognition of women in sport and balancing motherhood with elite competition.

Her legacy extends beyond medals — she redefined longevity in endurance sports, inspiring generations of Nordic athletes. In Norway, her name is synonymous with discipline and grace under pressure.

Even after retirement, Marit Bjørgen's tracks in the snow remain a guiding path for every athlete who dreams, dares, and endures.

Bonnie Blair – The Underdog Who Skated for Her Father

BONNIE BLAIR - THE UNDERDOG WHO SKATED FOR HER FATHER

Bonnie Blair's rise from an ordinary small-town girl to one of America's greatest Olympians, is a story of courage, loss, and unshakable will. Born in 1964 in Cornwall, New York, and raised in Champaign, Illinois, she grew up in a tight-knit, working-class family where skating was a shared passion. Her father, Charlie Blair, was the heart of that passion — a tireless supporter who drove her to local rinks and timed every practice lap from the sidelines. He believed she was destined for greatness, even when few others did.

Blair's first Olympic appearance at Sarajevo 1984 ended quietly, far from the podium. But she returned four years later at Calgary 1988 with fierce determination and a heavy heart. Just months before those Games, her beloved father passed away suddenly. Bonnie considered withdrawing, but her mother urged her to skate — "Do it for your dad."

In Calgary, she channelled her grief into glory, winning the 500 meters and dedicating her first gold medal to her father's memory. It was the beginning of one of the most extraordinary streaks in Winter Olympic history. At Albertville 1992 and Lillehammer 1994, she dominated again, claiming four more golds and one bronze, becoming the first American woman to win five Winter Olympic gold medals. Her remarkable consistency in sprint distances — where races are won or lost by hundredths of a second — earned her worldwide admiration.

Blair's success was even more remarkable considering her size and background. At 5'5", she lacked the powerful build of her European rivals, and she often trained with borrowed equipment or limited funding. Yet, through sheer perseverance, she became a symbol of American grit and grace. After retiring, Bonnie Blair turned her platform toward motivational speaking and humanitarian work, inspiring new generations with her father's lesson: *"Heart beats talent when talent forgets to have heart."*

Clas Thunberg – From Rowdy Rebel to Winter Olympic Royalty

When the first Winter Olympic Games took place in Chamonix, France, in 1924, a spirited Finn named Clas Thunberg emerged as one of sport's earliest global superstars. Known as much for his fiery temper and stubborn independence as for his unmatched talent on ice, Thunberg's journey from rebellious youth to five-time Olympic champion is one of transformation and triumph.

Born in Helsinki in 1893, Thunberg was far from the disciplined athlete he later became. As a young man, he was headstrong, fond of nightlife, and often dismissed as a troublemaker. But the lure of speed skating — the national pride of Finland — eventually gave him purpose. Under the guidance of coach Walter Jakobsson, Thunberg channelled his wild energy into the single-minded pursuit of perfection on ice.

At the 1924 Chamonix Winter Games, Thunberg dominated the competition, winning three gold medals, a silver, and a bronze. Four years later, at St. Moritz 1928, he returned to claim two more golds. In total, he amassed five Olympic gold medals and remains the only skater ever to win the "all-round" Olympic title, an event that combined all distances into one ultimate test of endurance and skill — a true reflection of his versatility.

Thunberg's success made him a national hero in Finland and a pioneer in the sport's professionalization. Known for his confidence (and occasional defiance of officials), he helped shape the bold, competitive spirit of future generations of skaters.

When asked late in life about his once-wild youth, Thunberg simply smiled and said, "A man must live with passion — only then can he skate with heart."

We invite you to watch this black and white film of the first ever Winter 1924 Olympics in Chamonix – France.

Sonja Henie (Norway, Figure Skating)
From Ice Queen to Silver Screen Star

Norwegian figure-skating legend Sonja Henie isn't just remembered for her three consecutive Olympic gold medals (1928, 1932, 1936) and ten straight world championships; her post-competitive career pivot into Hollywood stardom and fashion influence defines a fascinating chapter in sport-meets-show-business history.

After dominating the amateur ice rink, Henie turned professional in 1936 and swiftly signed with Twentieth Century-Fox. Her first feature film, *One in a Million* (1936), established her Hollywood presence — she went on to star in a string of box-office hits like *Thin Ice* (1937) and *My Lucky Star* (1938). In these films, her skating excellence, glamour, and choreography became central attractions. She became one of Hollywood's highest paid stars of her era. Henie's influence extended far beyond skating and film.

She pioneered the "white-skate boot" look, short skating skirts and a graceful, balletic style of skating attire that fused athleticism with feminine elegance. Her Hollywood image also enabled her to become a lifestyle brand: she appeared in endorsement deals, ice-revue tours and fashion-skating spectacles that helped popularise figure skating as both sport and entertainment.

By leveraging her athletic success into a broader entertainment and fashion platform, Sonja Henie helped transition figure skating into a mass-market spectacle. Her combination of competitive dominance,  film star charisma and fashion sensibility, made her a unique cultural icon of the 1930s and '40s.

 For any book examining Olympians who became influencers beyond sport, Henie's story is rich: sport → celebrity → style institution.

Eileen Gu (China/USA, Freestyle Skiing)

First freeskier to win three medals in a ingle Winter Games (2022)

At just 18 years old during the 2022 Winter Olympics in Beijing, Eileen Gu made headlines around the world—not only for her breathtaking athletic performance but for the broader questions her story raised about identity, nationality and sport. Born in San Francisco to an American father and a Chinese mother, Gu chose to compete for China beginning in 2019, a decision that generated global publicity and intense conversation.

On the snow, Gu delivered. She captured two gold medals—in big air and half-pipe—and a silver in slopestyle, becoming the youngest Olympic champion in her freestyle discipline and the first freeskier to win three medals in a single Winter Games. In one defining moment, Gu landed a daring double-cork 1620—an aerial manoeuvre few women had ever attempted in competition—and sealed her place in history.

Beyond the medals and tricks, what amplified Gu's global impact was the narrative that surrounded her. As a U.S.–born athlete representing China, her decision touched on sport and culture, East and West, belonging and ambition. She said of her dual identity: *"When I'm in the U.S., I'm American; when I'm in China, I'm Chinese."* The choice drew both admiration and scrutiny — some celebrated her as a bridge between nations, others questioned the implications amid geopolitical tensions.

Off the slopes, Gu rapidly became a media and commercial phenomenon: high-profile modelling campaigns, luxury brand endorsements, and a platform to inspire young athletes, especially girls, in China and beyond. Her story thus transcends sport—it's about identity, bold choices, and the cultures we represent.

Johannes Thingnes Bø – 5 Olympic Gold Medals

Johannes Thingnes Bø

He has won **nine** Olympic medals (including five golds).

Johannes has established himself as one of the modern greats of biathlon, combining extraordinary athletic achievement with a compelling off-track persona that resonates with fans and media alike. He is a Norwegian gold-medallist who has upheld his country's tradition of Nordic excellence — as recorded, he has won nine Olympic medals (including five golds) as part of his outstanding career.

From his mineral-sharp shooting to his rapid skiing and countless podiums, Johannes has become a fan favourite, not just in Scandinavia but around the world. His dominance in competition draws spectators in, but it's his approachable attitude and visible passion that deepen the connection.

Whether he's waving to his home crowd, celebrating joyfully after a win, or remaining composed after a near-miss, he presents the full spectrum of an athlete's emotional journey. Johannes' media presence extends beyond simply winning races. His interviews often reflect humility, humour and honesty — rare qualities among elite athletes who are often guarded in public. His visibility in European broadcast coverage, magazine features and social-media clips further amplifies his star quality. For broadcasters and sponsors alike, he represents the ideal blend of elite performance and personality.

Off-course, Johannes shows a grounded character. Whether interacting with fans after races, taking part in promotional or charitable activities, or simply reflecting on his career in media comments, he comes across as genuine and invested in more than just podiums. His camaraderie with teammates and respect for competitors add to his stature as a sportsman, rather than just a champion.

Toni Sailer – Extraordinary Olympian - National hero

Austrian alpine-skiing legend Toni Sailer rose to global fame and national hero status through his extraordinary performance at the 1956 Winter Olympics in Cortina d'Ampezzo, and his subsequent film and entertainment career.

At just 20 years old, Sailer swept all three alpine skiing events — downhill, giant slalom and slalom — at those Games, becoming the first athlete ever to win three gold medals in alpine skiing at a single Winter Olympics.

In Austria, where alpine skiing is much more than a sport, Sailer's achievement instantly elevated him into the realm of national icon. Nicknamed "The Blitz from Kitz," because it reflected his lightning-fast runs and Austria's high hopes.

His dominant victory margins (for example winning the giant slalom by over six seconds) highlighted an era-defining performance.

Beyond his medals, Sailer's impact in his homeland was cultural: his wins helped popularise alpine skiing both domestically and internationally, turning him into a symbol of Austrian ski excellence. He was honoured repeatedly, including being named Austria's Sportsman of the Year in 1956, 1957 and 1958.

After retiring from competitive skiing in 1959, Sailer transitioned into the entertainment world. He appeared in a string of films during the late 1950s and 1960s, often in Alpine settings that combined his athletic identity with on-screen charisma. His filmography includes titles such as *A Piece of Heaven* (1957) and *Twelve Girls and One Man* (1959).

These roles kept Sailer in the public eye beyond sport and reinforced his status as a multi-talented celebrity: athlete, actor and later even singer and entrepreneur.

Jean-Claude Killy: From the Slopes to the Boardroom

When the 1968 Winter Olympics were held in Grenoble, France, a young man from the French Alps captured the world's imagination.

Jean-Claude Killy achieved an extraordinary feat — winning gold in all three alpine skiing events: downhill, slalom, and giant slalom. His clean sweep made him an instant global superstar, the embodiment of French elegance, confidence, and athletic brilliance.

But what truly set Killy apart, was what came after his skiing triumphs. Instead of fading from public view, he demonstrated how an athlete could successfully transition from sporting hero to international businessman and marketing visionary. He became one of the first Winter Olympians to understand that fame could be transformed into a powerful personal brand.

In the years following Grenoble, Killy capitalized on his reputation by signing sponsorship deals, endorsing products, and starring in advertisements that reached millions. His charisma and credibility made him an ideal ambassador for luxury and sports brands alike. He also appeared in films and television, adding to his global recognition.

Killy later turned his focus to the business and administrative sides of sport. He became a key figure in sports marketing and event organization, notably serving as co-president of the organizing committee for the 1992 Winter Olympics in Albertville, France. Under his leadership, Albertville delivered one of the most modern, commercially successful Games of its era.

Through his post-sport achievements, Killy helped define the model of the modern athlete-entrepreneur. He showed that Olympic success could serve as a launchpad for influence in business, media, and global sport governance.

Tara Lipinski: Turning Olympic Gold into a Golden Career

When Tara Lipinski glided onto the ice at the 1998 Nagano Winter Olympics, she was just 15 years old — a teenager with dazzling talent, unshakable poise, and the determination of a champion.

Against a field of seasoned veterans, she delivered a flawless and emotional performance that captured the world's heart. Her gold medal made her the youngest individual Winter Olympic champion in history at the time, a record that cemented her place as a figure skating legend.

But Tara Lipinski's story didn't end at the podium. It was only the beginning of a remarkable transformation from athlete to media powerhouse. Understanding early that Olympic fame could open new doors, she built a career that showed how champions could reinvent themselves beyond sport.

After turning professional, Lipinski toured globally in ice shows, signed major endorsement deals, and became a familiar face in American popular culture. Her youthful energy and engaging personality made her a favourite guest on talk shows and commercials alike. Yet her most impressive reinvention came when she transitioned into broadcasting, turning her first-hand Olympic insight into a powerful storytelling tool.

Partnering with fellow Olympian Johnny Weir, Lipinski became one of NBC's most recognized figure skating commentators, offering sharp analysis, humour, and flair. The duo's chemistry and professionalism turned them into television icons, extending her influence to a new generation of fans.

Today, Tara Lipinski is not only remembered for her gold medal but also for her media savvy and business acumen. She exemplifies how athletes can leverage Olympic success into sustainable careers — not just in front of cameras, but as influential voices shaping how the world sees sport.

Kjetil Jansrud: The Comeback King of Norwegian Skiing

In the fast and unforgiving world of alpine skiing, few athletes embody resilience and determination quite like Kjetil Jansrud of Norway. Known for his mastery of the downhill and super-G events, Jansrud carved his name into Winter Olympic history not only through his gold-medal triumphs but also through his remarkable comebacks from injury — each time returning stronger, faster, and more determined than ever.

Born in 1985 in Stavanger, Jansrud emerged as part of Norway's golden generation of alpine skiers, alongside teammates like Aksel Lund Svindal. His technical skill, fearlessness, and calm precision on icy slopes made him a favourite in the speed events where risk is constant and mistakes are costly.

Jansrud's defining moment came at the 2014 Sochi Winter Olympics, where he claimed gold in the super-G and silver in the downhill, cementing his status as one of the sport's elites. He followed that with bronze in super-G at PyeongChang 2018, proving his longevity at the top level.

However, what truly sets Jansrud apart is not only his medal count but his tenacity in the face of adversity. Over the course of his career, he suffered multiple serious injuries — including a broken leg and torn knee ligaments — each threatening to end his time on the slopes. Yet each time, he fought back with trademark Norwegian grit, returning to win again on the World Cup circuit and inspire both teammates and fans.

Beyond the medals, Jansrud is celebrated for his sportsmanship and leadership. A role model for perseverance, he has shown that greatness isn't only measured in gold, but in the courage to keep rising after every fall. His story stands as a tribute to endurance, professionalism, and the unbreakable spirit that defines a true Olympian.

Oksana Masters: From Chernobyl's Shadow to Paralympic Glory

Oksana Masters' extraordinary life story is one of courage, resilience, and unbreakable will — a journey that began amid tragedy in Ukraine, in the lingering aftermath of the Chernobyl nuclear disaster. Born in 1989 with severe limb differences — missing both fibulas, with webbed fingers and other birth defects attributed to radiation exposure — she was abandoned at birth and spent her early childhood in orphanages under grim conditions.

Her life changed forever when she was adopted by an American single mother, Gay Masters, who brought her to the United States at age seven. After enduring years of surgeries and ultimately the amputation of both legs, Oksana discovered a new purpose through sport.

What began as a way to rebuild strength and confidence soon blossomed into a career that would make her one of the most decorated Paralympians in U.S. history.

Masters' athletic versatility is unmatched. She has competed — and medalled — in both Winter and Summer Paralympic Games, across Nordic skiing, biathlon, rowing, and cycling. At the Beijing 2022 Winter Paralympics, she captured multiple medals, solidifying her reputation as the leading star of Team USA. Her dominance extends to road cycling, where she claimed gold at the Tokyo 2020 Paralympics, proving that her determination knows no seasonal limits.

Yet beyond the medals, Oksana Masters represents something much greater. She is a symbol of survival and transformation — from a child born in the shadow of one of history's worst nuclear disasters to an international ambassador for hope and inclusion.

Her story is a reminder that adversity can forge champions, and that triumph often emerges from the darkest beginnings. Through her relentless spirit, compassion, and advocacy, Oksana Masters has become a living legend.

Brian McKeever: Canada's Vision of Greatness

Few athletes in Winter Paralympic history have achieved the remarkable combination of dominance, resilience, and humility displayed by Brian McKeever, the legendary Canadian Para Nordic skier.

Legally blind due to Stargardt's disease, a degenerative eye condition that began affecting his vision in his teens, McKeever went on to become the most decorated Canadian Winter Paralympian of all time, with an extraordinary tally of 20 medals — including 16 gold.

Born in Calgary, Alberta, McKeever's journey to greatness began on the snowy trails of Canmore, where he trained alongside his older brother Robin McKeever, himself an Olympian. When Brian's vision began to fade, his determination only grew stronger.

Together, the brothers forged one of the most successful partnerships in Paralympic history — Robin serving as Brian's guide skier, calling out directions, pacing, and navigating the challenging

Nordic courses that require strength, balance, and total trust.

McKeever first burst onto the Paralympic scene at Salt Lake City in 2002, winning two gold medals and setting the stage for a record-breaking career that would span six Paralympic Games. His continued dominance at Turin (2006), Vancouver (2010), Sochi (2014), PyeongChang (2018), and Beijing (2022) turned him into a national hero.

One of McKeever's most remarkable achievements came when he qualified for the able-bodied Canadian Olympic team for the 2010 Vancouver Games, after winning the national 50 km cross-country trials — a feat that highlighted his world-class talent.

Brian McKeever's story is not just about medals; it's about vision without sight — a story of perseverance, partnership, and pride that continues to inspire Canadians and athletes around the world.

Lauren Woolstencroft: Engineering Gold and Inspiring the World

In the history of Canadian Paralympic sport, few names shine as brightly as Lauren Woolstencroft, whose story of determination, excellence, and inspiration transcends the boundaries of sport.

Born without a left forearm and both legs below the knee, Woolstencroft refused to let physical challenges define her limits. Instead, she engineered one of the most extraordinary careers in Para Alpine skiing — and became a symbol of what's possible when talent meets tenacity.

At the 2010 Vancouver Paralympic Winter Games, competing on home snow, Woolstencroft delivered one of the most dominant performances in Paralympic history. She achieved a clean sweep of five gold medals across five Alpine disciplines — downhill, slalom, giant slalom, super combined, and super-G. No Canadian athlete, Olympian or

Paralympian, had ever accomplished such a feat at a single Games.

By the time she retired, she had amassed eight Paralympic gold medals in total — an unparalleled record that secured her place among Canada's greatest champions.

Off the slopes, Woolstencroft's journey continued to inspire. A professional electrical engineer, she brought the same precision and focus that powered her skiing career into her work in renewable energy and technology. Her story reached a global audience when Toyota featured her in its *"Good Odds"* Super Bowl commercial during the 2018 broadcast — a moving ad that chronicled her rise from a determined child to a Paralympic legend, concluding with the powerful tagline: "When you're free to move, anything is possible."

Woolstencroft's achievements have earned her numerous honours, including induction into the Greater Victoria Sports Hall of Fame in 2015.

Bibian Mentel-Spee: The Unbreakable Spirit of Paralympic Snowboarding

Few athletes have embodied resilience, courage, and grace under pressure like Bibian Mentel-Spee of the Netherlands. A trailblazer both on and off the slopes, Mentel-Spee not only helped establish para-snowboarding as a Paralympic sport but also achieved the extraordinary feat of winning gold medals at two Paralympic Games while fighting cancer multiple times.

Her story began long before her Paralympic triumphs. Originally a promising snowboarder on the Dutch national team, Bibian's career took a dramatic turn in 2001 when she was diagnosed with bone cancer, leading to the amputation of her lower leg. Rather than give up, she returned to snowboarding within months — determined to continue competing and to prove that life after amputation could still be powerful and fulfilling.

Her fighting spirit didn't stop there. Mentel-Spee became a key advocate for the inclusion of para-snowboarding in the Paralympic program, lobbying tirelessly for years. Thanks to her efforts, the sport made its debut at the Sochi 2014 Winter Paralympics, where she fittingly won gold in snowboard cross, marking a fairytale moment for both her and the sport she had championed.

Even as cancer returned repeatedly — nine diagnoses in total — Bibian refused to let it define her. At the PyeongChang 2018 Paralympics, already battling the disease again, she delivered one of the most inspiring performances in Paralympic history, capturing two gold medals in snowboard cross and banked slalom.

Mentel-Spee's legacy extends far beyond her medals. She founded the Mentelity Foundation, dedicated to helping young people with disabilities discover the joy and freedom of sport.

Bibian Mentel-Spee passed away in 2021, but her courage, optimism, and transformative impact continue to inspire generations — a true testament to the power of the human spirit.

Daniel Cnossen: From the Battlefield to the Podium

Few stories in Paralympic history reflect courage and transformation as powerfully as that of Daniel Cnossen, a former U.S. Navy SEAL who turned tragedy into triumph.

Once leading special operations missions in Afghanistan, Cnossen's life changed forever in 2009 during a night assault mission when he stepped on an improvised explosive device (IED). The blast took both of his legs above the knee and set him on a long, gruelling path of recovery — both physical and mental.

After more than 40 surgeries and two years of rehabilitation, Cnossen refused to be defined by what he had lost. Instead, he focused on what he could still achieve. His warrior discipline, resilience, and mental toughness carried over from the battlefield to the snowfields, where he took up Para Nordic skiing and biathlon — sports that demand strength, precision, and endurance.

At the PyeongChang 2018 Winter Paralympic Games, Daniel Cnossen made history. He captured gold in the men's 7.5 km sitting biathlon, becoming the first American man to win biathlon gold at either the Olympics or Paralympics. His performance didn't stop there — he went on to win six more medals in cross-country skiing and biathlon, earning a total of seven medals across multiple events. His achievements were not just about athletic success but about redefining what is possible through perseverance and purpose.

Beyond sport, Cnossen has become one of the world's most respected motivational and leadership speakers. Drawing on his experiences as a SEAL officer, a combat survivor, and a Paralympic champion, he now inspires audiences with his message of resilience, adaptability, and leadership under pressure.

Daniel Cnossen's journey is a living example of the human capacity to overcome. From the ashes of combat injury to the heights of Paralympic glory, he continues to prove that even when life changes in an instant, greatness can still be achieved — one determined stride at a time.

Oleksandra Kononova – The Orphan Who Skied into a Nation's Heart

Few stories in Paralympic history capture the power of resilience like that of Oleksandra Kononova, the Ukrainian skier who transformed tragedy into triumph. Born in Brovary, Ukraine, Kononova lost the use of her right arm after a childhood illness and grew up in poverty, orphaned and raised by her grandmother.

Her path to sport was anything but certain — yet through sheer determination, she rose to become one of the brightest stars of the Vancouver 2010 Paralympic Winter Games.

At just 19 years old, Kononova astonished the world with her dominance on snow, capturing three gold medals — in the 12.5 km Standing Biathlon, the 5 km Classic Cross-Country Ski, and the Sprint Classic — as well as a silver medal for good measure. Her remarkable debut earned her the Best Games Debut Award at the 2011 Paralympic Sport Awards, and back home she was named Ukraine's Sports Personality of the Year — the first Paralympian ever to receive that honour.

Kononova's backstory made her achievements even more poignant. As a child, she lacked access to proper equipment or training facilities and often trained in second-hand gear. Yet, her spirit and optimism caught the attention of national coaches, who saw not only raw talent but fierce willpower. By the time she arrived in Vancouver, she was ready to prove that disability could never define destiny.

Beyond medals, Kononova became a symbol of hope for thousands of young Ukrainians with disabilities, showing that courage and persistence can rewrite any story. Her humility and grace off the track matched her strength on it.

As she prepared for Sochi 2014, Oleksandra Kononova carried more than her country's flag — she carried its heart.

Hermann Maier – The Iron Man of Alpine Skiing

Few athletes in Winter Olympic history embody resilience and raw power like Hermann Maier, the Austrian alpine skier whose career became a symbol of courage, comeback, and uncompromising determination.

Born in 1972 in Flachau, Austria, Maier was not considered a prodigy. Too small and physically undeveloped as a teenager, he was rejected from the Austrian national ski academy. Instead, he worked as a bricklayer and trained in his spare time, carving out his own rugged path to the top of world skiing.

Maier burst into global fame at the 1998 Nagano Winter Olympics, where he delivered one of the most unforgettable moments in Olympic history. During the downhill event, he lost control at over 100 km/h, flew spectacularly off the course, flipped through the air, and crashed violently into a safety net — a fall so dramatic it became an instant worldwide headline. Yet in a display of astonishing toughness, Maier walked away, returned to the starting gate two days later, and won two Olympic gold medals in the Super-G and Giant Slalom.

This combination of fearlessness and skill earned him the nickname "The Herminator." Over the following years, Maier dominated the World Cup circuit, winning four overall titles, three Super-G titles, six giant slalom titles, and more than 50 individual World Cup races. His powerful, aggressive style redefined modern alpine skiing.

Just as remarkable as his rise was his comeback. In 2001, Maier suffered a near-fatal motorcycle accident that shattered his leg and threatened not only his career but his mobility. Doctors doubted he would walk normally again. Instead, Maier fought through a long, painful rehabilitation and returned to competition — a comeback widely regarded as one of the greatest in sports history.

Against all expectations, he qualified for the 2006 Turin Winter Olympics, winning silver in the Super-G and bronze in the giant slalom, proving to the world once again that his spirit was unbreakable.

Hermann Maier's legacy lives on not only in medals but in the message, he embodied: *fall hard, rise harder!*

Winter Olympic Cities

1924 - Chamonix, FRANCE
1928 - St. Moritz, SWITZERLAND
1932 - Lake Placid, USA
1936 - Garmisch-Partenkirchen, GERMANY

1940 - The 1940 Winter Olympics were cancelled due to World War II.

1944 - The 1944 Winter Olympics were also cancelled due to World War II.
1948 - St. Moritz, SWITZERLAND
1952 - Oslo, NORWAY
1956 - Cortina d'Ampezzo, ITALY
1960 - Squaw Valley, USA
1964 - Innsbruck, AUSTRIA
1968 - Grenoble, FRANCE
1972 - Sapporo, JAPAN
1976 - Innsbruck, AUSTRIA
1980 - Lake Placid, USA
1984 - Sarajevo, YUGOSLAVIA
1988 - Calgary, CANADA
1992 - Albertville, FRANCE
1994 - Lillehammer, NORWAY
1998 - Nagano, JAPAN
2002 - Salt Lake City, USA
2006 - Turin, ITALY
2010 - Vancouver, CANADA
2014 - Sochi, RUSSIA
2018 - Pyeongchang, SOUTH KOREA
2022 - Beijing, CHINA
2018 - Pyeongchang, SOUTH KOREA
2022 - Beijing, CHINA
2026 - Milano-Cortina, ITALY
2030 - French Alps
2034 - Salt Lake City – UTAH – USA

"I hope you enjoyed Chasing Winter Gold. We had a lot of fun getting it together. It was almost as much fun as winter sports!"

**Jess Bridger
Co-Author**

BY THE SAME AUTHOR:

HOW TO DEVELOP A MEMORY LIKE AN ELEPHANT."

Have you ever forgotten a name in less that 3 seconds after you have been introduced? Have you ever been to the Supermarket planning to buy six items and only been able to remember four when you arrived? Have you ever 'lost' your keys, wallet, purse or the TV remote control in your own home?

If so, perhaps it's not because you have a bad memory. Perhaps it is because you were never taught *how* to remember.

At school we were taught the three R's: **r**eading, '**r**iting and '**r**ithmatic. Very few schools taught the 4th and probably the most important R: **R**emembering!

If you would like to improve your memory, check out my book by scanning the QR code.

THE 'INSPIRATIONAL' QR CODE:
One of the most inspirational things that has ever happened to me was when a friend's father said, "Max, I want to thank you, as I feel you may have saved my son's life." He was talking about a video I posted on the Internet titled, *"Only 17."*

As 'speed' is the main cause of most teenager car crashes, this YouTube video is designed to encourage teenagers to drive slower. You may wonder what 'credibility' I have, to post such a video about a car crash. Believe me – as a victim of a near fatal car crash myself – I have the required credibility!

My Dad used to say, *"Showing is better than telling!"* Hence, I invite you to scan the QR code at right to see and hear the story. And I'm hoping you will **take a picture of the QR code** and send it onto someone who has teenage children. And perhaps one day someone will say to you, *"I want to thank you, as I feel you may have saved my child's life."*
Now that's inspiring!

A Closing Reflection

Baron Pierre de Coubertin, the founder of the modern Olympic Games, dreamed that sport would be the glue that binds humanity together, forging connections across nations and cultures. This Edgar Guest verse below (published around 1915) carries that same timeless truth: that through our kindness, our actions, and our respect for one another—both in life and in sport—we can help shape a better, more united world.

IS ANYBODY HAPPIER...

Is anybody happier because you passed their way
Does anyone remember that you spoke with them today
Were you selfish pure and simple as you rushed along your way
Or is someone mighty grateful for a deed you did today

Can you say tonight in parting with the day that's slipping past
That you helped a single human in the many that you passed
Is a single heart rejoicing over what you did or said
Can a person whose hopes were fading now with courage look ahead

Did you waste a day or lose it, was it well or poorly spent
Did you leave a trail of kindness or a scar of discontent
When you close your eyes in slumber, do you think your God will say
You have earned one more tomorrow for the deeds you did today

A message from Max & Jess

We know there are many inspirational stories missing from these pages and we extend our apologies to all Olympic and Paralympic athletes not included in the pages of our books. If you are a Summer Olympian, Winter Olympian, Paralympian, or just a sports fan, like us, we would love to hear your inspirational story.

Please send it to max@hitchins.com.au or check out our website ChasingGold.com.au. Perhaps we can include your story on our website and/or in an upcoming book.

PS - If you enjoyed this book, you may like a previous book I wrote called CHASING GOLD. See (link to Amazon)

www.ingramcontent.com/pod-product-compliance
Lightning Source LLC
Chambersburg PA
CBHW051438290426
44109CB00016B/1601